Phantom of the sea . . .

As the ship moves into view on a northeasterly course, with every rag of canvas her three masts can carry, a deathlike silence reigns over the crowd of spectators who cannot believe what they are seeing. Why does she move so fast, even when no wind is blowing? ̶ aze, her outline ̶ ose running alo ̶ an- not keep up ̶ ̶ ̶ ̶ ̶

Soon, omi ̶ along her heeling ̶ ̶ ̶ ̶ ̶ ̶ ̶ ̶ ̶ ̶ y, the phantom vessel shudde ̶ ̶ ̶ hough she has run aground. Shadowy forms are running along her length. But before any of them reach their goal, the vessel is engulfed in flames. Burning top masts and yard-arms crash to her decks. Obscure figures begin to jump over her sides. Then, as the spectral ship becomes engulfed in flames from stem to stern, she plunges bow-first down into the black waters— and the night is black once again. . . .

GHOST SHIPS

True Stories of Nautical Nightmares, Hauntings, and Disasters

RICHARD WINER

BERKLEY BOOKS, NEW YORK

GHOST SHIPS

A Berkley Book / published by arrangement with
Flying "W" Incorporated

PRINTING HISTORY
Berkley edition / July 2000

ISBN: 0-425-17548-0

BERKLEY®
Berkley Books are published by The Berkley Publishing Group,
a division of Penguin Putnam Inc., 375 Hudson Street,
New York, New York 10014.
BERKLEY and the ''B'' design
are trademarks belonging to Penguin Putnam Inc.

PRINTED IN THE UNITED STATES OF AMERICA

10 9 8 7 6 5 4 3 2 1

This book is dedicated to all of those American sailors who have gone down to the sea in ships.

CONTENTS

INTRODUCTION

S ince man first pushed off from shore in his hollowed-out log onto a sea pervaded with great white sharks and other perpetually hungry flesh-eating creatures and was fortunate enough to reach dry land again, there have been tales about the sea and its perils. They have varied from the sinister fate just beyond the far horizon to creatures that lunge up from the depths with jaws gaping large enough to swallow an entire ship.

Sea stories rarely fail to enthrall the listener. Many, even today, have been mere figments of the imagination that have become more imaginative with each telling. Others had some element of truth to begin with but have nonetheless been expanded on with each telling.

In fact, most stories of the sea, especially those with a strange and fateful twist, have been so distorted that they fall well into the realm of the unbelievable.

But for every thousand or so contrived or totally distorted tales of the sea, there is at least one story, one happening, with enough documented facts to be completely believable . . . believable, even for the most sagacious skeptic.

Yes, the sea is a place of many mysteries. It swarms with secrets. People know less about the sea floor than about the surface of the moon. And soon we will know more about Mars than what awaits us a dozen or so miles beneath the surface of the ocean. Possibly, when the day arrives when submersible vehicles are capable of scouring the sea bottom in its entirety, there will no longer be any mysteries of the sea—except those we conceive ourselves. But until then, it will continue to abound with the incredible effects of the unknown.

I first became interested in the mysteries of the sea while warming a bar stool in Kowloon, which is just across the bay from Hong Kong. In 1967, Kowloon, unlike Hong Kong, was still a place of intrigue and mystery. Mike's waterfront bar was very offbeat, a place unmentioned by tourist guides. The establishment was a rough, very rough, joint. It was a saloon or pub, where if you were not a regular, you just minded your own business and didn't complain about the stale pretzels or watered-down drinks. The bulk of Mike's clientele consisted of weathered British seamen with a scattering of beached Americans who, for one reason or another, were unable to return to the States. How I ended up at Mike's Place I cannot remember. Possibly, I had a little too much alcohol before drifting away from the main streets of Kowloon. At the time, I had been gradually working my way home after filming a documentary in Viet Nam.

Although fights and near fights were common at Mike's, most of the strife and rivalry was verbal. Mike's bar, however, did have a good element or two. When old sailors begin to talk, sea stories are sure to evolve. And a few of them might have given Jack London and Joseph Conrad a run for the money. The fascinating thing, though, was that some of the yarns, told by those old sea dogs, actually contained more than just a grain of truth. The names, places and times, more often than not, matched up, for those old salts had been through it all.

In fact, it was at Mike's Place that I first heard of an area of ocean off the southeastern coast of Florida where ships would steam seaward, not to be seen again; aircraft flew over the eastern horizon never to come back; and yachts simply vanished without any trace whatsoever. My sojourn to Mike's Place planted a seed within my mind that later became an award-winning documentary film narrated by the late Vincent Price and a *New York Times* bestseller about the Bermuda Triangle. Both were titled *The Devil's Triangle*.

When a story of the sea is regaled by an old leather-skinned, half-drunk old salt, it comes to life, as though its action were leaping right out at you. In spite of the smell of stale whiskey and pungent tobacco smoke, those orators of the ocean verbally took their listeners to sea. I don't believe that any other place in the world possessed a saltier ambience. One minute the orator would be shouting out his parables, and the next second he would be whispering as though he wanted only you alone to hear his words. As you listened to those old sailors, you could feel the roll of the sea and taste the salt water.

In the following pages, I have put down in print a collection of twentieth-century mysteries of the sea. Some are fully authenticated by witnesses. Others depend mostly on documents. And a few, from the narrators at Mike's, appear to be only partly substantiated. Whatever. I believe that you, the reader, will find all of them as exciting as I have. Let me give you a few clips of what awaits you in the pages ahead:

It's not very frequent that the United States Navy admits that the disappearance of one of its own supply ships has become the subject of the greatest mystery of the sea ever, or that one of its own destroyers was a ghost ship playing a strange, spectral role during World War II—on the side of the enemy.

There have been documented instances of vessels carrying a curse from launching to their watery grave, such as the one featured in a 1937 issue of *Life* magazine.

And which ship, may I ask you, was the unluckiest and most jinxed warship of World War II? I'll give you a clue. It was a battleship, a vessel that should have been invulnerable to hexes, jinxes, and other supernatural afflictions.

And I want to tell you about certain steamships, steamers so cursed that no crew would man them—vessels sailors called "death ships."

And what collection of nautical nightmares would be complete without reporting about the ghosts of John Wayne and Errol Flynn, seen pacing the decks of their respective yachts?

I hope that by now I have whetted your nautical appetite and lust for the unknown enough for you to charge into the pages that follow. I wish you happy reading and smooth sailing.

ONE

The Ship of Doom

The north wind was exploding down Russia's Pacific coast as it always does in winter. Yet the night was clear and star bright. The winter of 1907 seemed particularly rugged in the northwestern Pacific. At the windswept port of Vladivostok, a number of ships, both sail and steam, were riding it out at anchor. One ship, however, stood out from the other vessels. From stem to stern she was engulfed in a fiery, wind-driven inferno. The appalling glow from the doomed vessel, casting an eerie orange light on nearby ships, was visible from as far as ten miles inland and beyond that distance from the sea. Onlookers, in dozens of small wave-tossed boats circling the flaming mass, made no effort to fight the fire. Nor had any of them attempted to prevent the fire when it first erupted. There was elation and merriment amongst them; they shouted with joy at the death of that ship. Some sang. Others, their arms protruding from seal-skin sleeves, toasted the inferno with bottles of vodka. They were cheering the doomed ship's demise.

For they knew that the vessel was diabolic—a death ship possessed by an unknown force of evil—a malevolent maritime malediction from which there was no escape for those who dared sail aboard it.

The *Ivan Vassili* was built in 1897 at St. Petersburg. Her hull was built of riveted iron plates; but the decks and superstructure were of wood. The ship had been designed for the sole purpose of carrying freight from one port to another. For propulsion, she was driven by a single triple-expansion steam engine. Her bunkers carried enough coal for 2500 miles of steaming at eight knots.

The *Ivan Vassili* was not one of those so-called cursed or hexed ships that carry a jinx from the day they are launched. No mishaps occurred at her launching, which was not on a Friday the thirteenth. Her maiden voyage had been uneventful. She possessed the same name from the day her keel was put down. There is no record of a curse ever having been placed on the ship. In fact, there was no reason, whatsoever, for the *Ivan Vassili* to become a seagoing calamity of horror and death.

For five uneventful years, the freighter plied the waters of the Baltic Sea and Gulf of Finland. Then in 1903, as the Russian Empire was making preparations for her disastrous war with Japan, the *Ivan Vassili* was ordered to carry a cargo of war materials to Vladivostok in advance of squadrons of Russian warships that were to follow.

The steamer's passage took her through the North Sea, into the Atlantic, and southward along the west coast of Africa. After coaling at Capetown, the *Ivan Vassili* steamed north along the east coast of Africa to Zanzibar, where she topped off her coal bunkers and loaded sacks of extra coal on her decks for the long, sweltering voyage across the Indian Ocean. Up to this point, everything had appeared normal as the steamer plied onward. On the journey across the Indian Ocean, however, the crew sensed that something was not right aboard their ship. No one could pinpoint what it was, but everyone was aware that some sort of invisible force was accompanying them. Men on deck watch during the sultry equatorial nights would suddenly feel a chill in the air. Others had feelings that someone was standing next to them when they were alone. Then, one evening, a group of men, relaxing just before the change of watch, saw something that left them in a state of traumatic shock. It was a luminous, nearly transparent apparition that appeared almost human in form. It walked across the deck and disappeared behind a lifeboat.

It was not until just before the *Ivan Vassili* reached Port Arthur, a military base leased by Russia from China, that whatever it was that seemed to be possessing the ship began taking its toll.

On the night before the vessel was to enter port, a deckhand suddenly let forth with a horrifying scream. Panic prevailed. Most of the crew went berserk. For twenty minutes, the men ran amuck, screaming wildly, racing about the ship, totally oblivious to what they were doing. They were beating each other and themselves. During the frenzied melee a seaman named Alec Govinski, broke away from the others, hurled himself over the rail into the blackness of the sea and disappeared. Then, in a matter of seconds, it was all over. Everything, including the possessed seamen, returned to normal. Except for the loss of Govinski, it was as if nothing had happened.

After the coaling stop at Port Arthur, the *Ivan Vassili* began the last leg of her passage to Vladivostok. Nothing unusual happened the first day out. The second day at sea was also uneventful. But on the third night, the crew was once again overwhelmed by whatever it was that seemed to possess their ship. After the delirium, screaming, and hysteria had subsided, the men collapsed on the deck. Then they discovered that another of their shipmates had disappeared during their orgy of terror. He, too, had apparently thrown himself overboard.

When the *Ivan Vassili* reached Vladivostok, a dozen crewmen attempted to desert, even before the cargo hatches were opened. All were rounded up and returned to the vessel. Soldiers kept the ship under surveillance to guard against further attempts to desert.

After being unloaded, the *Ivan Vassili* put to sea for Hong Kong. The passage was a maritime nightmare. Four times, the ship was gripped by terror and trauma during the voyage south. After each of the first two incidents, a crewman committed suicide. During the third occurrence, a stoker died of fright. The fourth incident took place as the steamer approached Hong Kong Harbor. Just hours from port, the captain, Sven Andrist, flung himself overboard from the flying bridge and drowned.

After docking at Hong Kong, the entire crew, with the exception of the second officer, Christ Hansen, and five Scandinavian seamen, deserted. Hansen took over as captain, replenished the crew with Chinese and Lascar seamen, and steamed for Sydney, Australia. The voyage south was uneventful until just one night out of Sydney, when Christ Hansen shot himself to death.

Even before the *Ivan Vassili*'s dock lines were secured, the crew began deserting. All except boatswain Harry Nelson fled ashore and melted into the populace a Sydney. With the help of Nelson, the company agents found a captain who didn't believe in ghosts. It took nearly four months, however, before an entire crew could be recruited—a crew that had never heard of the goings-on that had plagued the ship.

The *Ivan Vassili* put to sea, bound for San Francisco with a cargo of wool. Within a week, the ship fell under another bout of terror. Two seamen went mad and had to be confined. Both were dead by the next morning. The following day, the captain, who didn't believe in ghosts, placed the barrel of a loaded revolver in his mouth and pulled the trigger. The crew refused to go on with the voyage. With the help of the first mate and those of the crew who still maintained some semblance of sanity, Harry Nelson put the ship about and headed for Vladivostok.

Upon their arrival back in the Russian city, the entire crew, including Harry Nelson, walked off the ship. Incentives, rewards and bonuses—all failed to get a crew for the *Ivan Vassili*. No one wanted any part of the death ship.

For years the *Ivan Vassili* strained at her anchor in the harbor. Not even a watchman could be found who was willing to spend a night aboard the ship of horror.

"Fire," said the men of Vladivostok who made their living from the sea, "is the only way to destroy the evil that has possessed that ship of doom!" And fire it was.

They watched the burning bridge topple into the flame engulfing the Number Two hold. As the iron skin of the ship began to buckle, the *Ivan Vassili*, still ablaze, was cast off from her mooring and dragged out to sea behind a tugboat.

The innards of the hull were still smoldering the next morning as she began rolling to starboard. The roll was slow at first, but gradually increased until the ship flipped over on its side and started to slide beneath the windswept surface. The men aboard the tug swore that just before the ship of death began its plunge, they heard an eerie, blood-curdling scream emanating from the flooding hulk. Whatever the source of evil was that possessed the *Ivan Vassili*, no one will ever know.

The *Ivan Vassili*'s calamitous career was not an isolated situation. There have been dozens of similar incidents aboard other ships. Many occurred before the twentieth century and, therefore, have not been included in this book, but others happened since 1900.

There was the 2,000 ton *Hinemoa* that succumbed to a storm in 1908 and washed ashore as a total wreck, ending a sixteen-year history of maritime malediction. On her maiden voyage in 1892, while en route from Scotland to New York, four ordinary seamen died of typhoid fever. On that same passage, her captain went insane. The *Hinemoa*'s second captain turned to a life of crime and died in prison. The third captain was fired by the owners as an alcoholic. The fourth captain was found dead in his bunk on his first trip aboard the vessel. Suicide at sea was the fate of the fifth captain. Under the command of the sixth captain, she capsized.

The *Hinemoa* was later salvaged and placed back in service. Under her seventh captain, two seamen were washed overboard and lost. Finally, in 1908, she was wrecked. The records do not state whether or not her loss occurred while under the command of her eighth captain.

For many years during the early part of this century, the hulk of an old sailing ship lay rotting at dockside in Bathurst, New Brunswick. Old-timers described her as having been an excellent, fully found vessel when she was first left at that dock. The ship, named *Squando*, had been abandoned to the elements because her owners were unable to find a crew to sail her. The old sea dogs who hung around the Bathurst waterfront felt that the *Squando* was haunted as the result of an eerie incident that occurred aboard her many years earlier.

On a summer night in 1899, the *Squando*, then under the Norwegian flag, was docked in San Francisco. The captain and his wife became enraged during a drunken brawl with the chief mate. During the fracas, the captain overpowered the mate and tied him to the mizzen mast. The captain's wife, infuriated and shrieking for vengeance, ripped a fire axe from its bracket and hacked away at the mate until his shattered head plopped to the deck. Both the captain and his wife received long prison terms.

A new captain took over the *Squando*. On his first voyage, he was killed during an attempted mutiny. The next captain died from unknown causes while at sea. Then another captain succumbed to fever at sea. After his death, no crew would sign aboard the *Squando*, and the vessel was permanently berthed at her final mooring. But odd happenings continued aboard the *Squando*. Watchmen guarding the ship reported strange goings-on—such as marlin spikes flying through the air, eerie voices, banging doors and even a headless man pacing the decks.

It wasn't long before even watchmen refused to stay aboard the vessel at night. Vandals and thieves steered clear of her. Thus, the *Squando* was left to rot at her moorings.

TWO

Without a Trace

"Disappeared without a trace." That eerie phrase applies to more vessels than the average person is likely to believe. To list both nineteenth- and twentieth-century disappearances would require several thick volumes simply to depict those of which we are aware. Vanishing at sea was more common during the 1800s for several reasons: lack of radio communications; less accurate navigation charts and instruments; more wooden and fewer seaworthy ships; unreliable storm predictions; slower ships, requiring longer periods at sea between ports; fewer laws governing safety at sea; and piracy.

During the twentieth century, however, when maritime electronics gradually became commonplace, boats and ships continued to head out onto the open sea, never to be seen again. Even with improved search and rescue techniques, radios on all vessels, near perfect navigation charts, sonar and depth finders, radar, sideband devices, and space-age satellite instrumentation—the unexplainable losses continue. They include every kind of vessel from obscure little West Indian fishing boats to sleek racing craft and even modern tankers and cargo ships.

Of course, storms, especially typhoons, account for some. One case involved the large three-masted passenger schooner *Fantom*, which vanished in 1998, while trying to outrun Hurricane Mitch in the western Caribbean. Receiving word of the approaching hurricane, the vessel put her hundred or so passengers ashore in Honduras. After consulting with the owners in Miami, the captain and owners felt the ship could better ride out Mitch on the open ocean rather than in port. The captain and the crew of thirty put to sea with the hope of outrunning the approaching storm. The *Fantom* was never heard from again. Coast guard search craft found a life jacket and a scant quantity of wreckage from the lost schooner.

Such weather conditions can be blamed for some vessels that are "lost without a trace." There have been many ships and yachts that have disappeared, however, never to be seen again, during fair weather, even within sight of shore or other craft.

The *Island Queen* was a picturesque, eighty-five foot staysail schooner. She was one of those sailing ships that, with all sails set and reaching into a fair breeze, brought adoration from all who beheld her. Wherever she called, throughout the Caribbean, crowds thronged to see her. In addition to her sail power, the *Island Queen* carried an auxiliary gasoline engine, which could push her along at six knots as she carried passengers and mail between the various islands of the eastern Caribbean.

Around 5:00 P.M. on August 4, 1944, the *Island*

Queen cast off from Grenada, bound for St. Vincent, the next island to the north. It was a short passage, during which one island would come in view before the other was out of sight. There was joy and merriment aboard the schooner, for most of the seventy-five passengers, including a number of women and children, were en route to a wedding party on St. Vincent.

Another big schooner, the black-hulled *Providence Mark*, was sailing in the company with the *Island Queen*. The weather was perfect—light southeasterly winds, a smooth sea, billowing sails, and a full moon. The two schooners made a race out of the voyage and were sailing neck and neck. At about 10:00 P.M., as they were off the eastern tip of Carriacou, a light, windless rain shower passed over the two ships. Just before the *Island Queen* entered the shower, those aboard the *Providence Mark* saw the other vessel flash her lights, but they thought it was part of the game.

When the black-hulled sailing vessel emerged from the shower, the *Island Queen* was nowhere to be seen. Everyone assumed that she had pulled out ahead and on into the night. The *Providence Mark* arrived at St. Vincent shortly before midnight. But the *Island Queen* wasn't there. When she still hadn't arrived by daylight, a search commenced. Both the United States and British navies participated. The quest for the missing vessel covered much of the Caribbean. But no trace whatsoever was found of the *Island Queen* or of the passengers and crew who were aboard her.

A number of theories were offered to explain why she disappeared. Fire was the first advanced, but that was discounted, for the flames at night would have been seen by those aboard the *Providence Mark* or from one of the islands, and there was no distress call radioed. Some suggested that waterspout had overwhelmed the *Island Queen*, but conditions that night were unfavorable for that to have happened. Others proposed U-boat action, but after Germany surrendered, it was discovered that only one German submarine was in the Caribbean area at the time—U-530, Lieutenant Lang commanding. The U-530 survived the war. But there was no mention in her logs or war diaries of her encountering or sinking a schooner.

The schooner *Island Queen* had become another unsolved mystery of the sea.

The history of Japanese seafaring abounds with legends of sea monsters, demons, and ghost ships. The crew of the freighter *Raifuku Maru* no doubt congratulated themselves when they signed aboard in January 1921 for a voyage that would take them far away from the frigid waters surrounding their homeland, to the Gulf Stream–warmed waters of the Caribbean and the tropical Atlantic—and presumably on to New York.

The *Raifuku Maru* made an uneventful passage across the Pacific, through the Panama Canal, and into the Caribbean. But as the ship steamed past the Bahamas, the Japanese crew found that strange happenings were more than mere legend in the waters of the western Atlantic, for the last that were ever heard from the *Raifuku Maru* was the Morse code message: "Danger like dagger now. Come Quick!" Then silence.

What happened to the Japanese ship? During the first half of 1921, at least ten other large ships disappeared in the western Atlantic. No less than six of them had sailed from Newport News, never to be heard from again.

There was some speculation of mass piracy. But if the *Raifuku Maru* had been attacked by pirates, the simple word "pirates" would have been faster and simpler to transmit. A UFO? Witnesses have described saucers, ovals, and cigar-shaped UFOs—but never one resembling a dagger.

One possibility that is more likely than any other explanation is a waterspout—a tornado at sea. There are differences of opinions among meteorologists as to the destructive force of a waterspout. To witness one is a striking experience. But to be aboard a vessel that encounters one is almost beyond description.

This writer experienced just such an episode some years ago on a voyage through subtropical seas aboard a small interisland tramp ship. The holds were crammed with concrete blocks, steel beams, and sacks of cement. The deck cargo consisted of tiers of lumber secured by chains made taught with chain tighteners and turnbuckles. The cargo was destined for a tourist resort being constructed on a privately owned West Indian island.

For the previous two days, sea conditions had been ideal. Eight- to ten-knot trade winds had made sitting under the awning aft of the wheelhouse most relaxing. But abruptly the breeze seemed to diminish. The ship's wake was creating the only blemish on the mirrorlike surface of the sea. Our speed, less than six knots, barely created any awareness of air movement. I could sense that the stifling heat was making everyone aboard the Honduran ship quite ill at ease.

Ahead to the southeast, a scattered line of gray clouds was forming. Soon, the darkening clouds began massing into one. Their upper layers appeared to be reaching almost into the stratosphere, where they began to spread out into an anvil shape. The lower fringe was almost perfectly horizontal except for an occasional saw-toothed edge struggling to reach the ocean's surface. In a matter of minutes, one of the fang-shaped edges slowly, very slowly, extended down toward the surface of the sea. The ship was moving closer, and the fang was directly in our track. Lower and lower it reached but it no longer resembled a fang. Surrounded by a blackening sky, its new shape was taking on the form of a dagger blade. Almost touching the water, it stopped. The ship continued to move closer. Then, like an illusionist's chimera, another dagger was emerging up out of the sea reaching toward the first one. They merged into a single body, reaching down out of the heavens.

Pausing momentarily, the gray-white dagger started to move across the water. The awe-inspiring spectacle had so mesmerized me that only then did I realize the captain must turn the ship, for the freighter was on a collision course with the swirling funnel.

The skipper's perpetual uniform consisted of rubber thong sandals, knee-length beltless khaki shorts that seemed to defy gravity unless they were held up by the huge wrinkle under his potbelly, and a battered officer's cap with the word "Captain" in gold braid above the visor. The cap must have survived numerous storms, voyages, and barroom brawls. The Honduran master, however, impressed me as being a bundle of seagoing joviality. But within this fat-faced little man was a streak of stubbornness.

The ship was maintaining its course, and so was the tornado of the sea. I could hear the helmsman screaming at the captain, who responded by shaking his head with disapproval. We were on a collision track! A confrontation between man and nature was rapidly becoming inevitable. It was too late to turn. The steady rumble of the ancient diesel was drowned out by a roar of the tornado. Except for the captain and helmsman, I was the only one still topside. The rest of the crew had fled below. The man at the wheel was tightening his grip on the spokes as I moved into the wheelhouse. In defiance of the captain, the helmsman suddenly spun the wheel hard to the starboard. A single fear overwhelmed all of my thoughts. Would we escape that seagoing tornado?

Still, the captain remained out on the wing bridge. Could he have been paralyzed with terror? The roar had become the sound of an express train bearing down on us. No, it was the sound of a dozen jet planes. Visibility disappeared into whiteness. It was as if the vessel had sailed right under the cataract of Niagara Falls. Something was happening out on deck. I couldn't tell what. Where was the captain? Was he swept overboard?

In less than half a minute, the cascade was gone, and the sea ahead was back to normal, but not the ship. The lumber that had been on deck was gone—floating in the sea astern, leaving an expanding trail across the sunlit ocean as the twisting victor of the encounter changed shape in the distance.

A number of hatch covers were also gone. The vessel's main deck railings were twisted masses of pipe. The thousand-pound cargo booms had been lifted out of their cradles and dropped onto the deck. The awning was not shredded—it was completely gone, to the last thread. The captain, bloodied and naked, was sitting on the bridge deck, his arms and legs wrapped around a stanchion. Smiling, he commented on how fresh the water tasted. The rest of that afternoon and the following day were spent recovering lumber and cargo hatches from the sea. I had been through a waterspout.

Like the sea itself, waterspouts are unpredictable. There have been incidents of ships coming in contact with them and surviving unscathed, while other vessels have succumbed to these seagoing tornados. Theodolite measurements have documented evidence of waterspouts attaining heights in excess of eight thousand feet, with shafts measuring fifteen hundred feet across. Once, when cruising in my sailboat, the *Running Bowline,* off Walker's Key at the north end of the Bahamas, I saw three waterspouts at one time. The coast guard once reported that one of its cutters had seen as many as nine at once.

Could the Japanese crew of the *Raifuku Maru*—never before having seen waterspouts—have described the vortex of a waterspout, because of panic and language barrier, as "like dagger?"

During the 1920s, like a plague, so many ships seemed to just disappear, leaving little or no evidence that they ever existed. For example, in 1921, a record number of ships vanished during the year's first three months. The list reads like a U-boat commander's war diary.

In February 1921, the Italian steamship *Monte San Michele*; the British steamer *Esperanza de Larringa*; the Brazilian cargo ship *Cabedallo*; the British tanker *Ottowa*; the sulphur ship *Hewitt*; and three Norwegian barks, the *Florino*, the *Svartskog*, and the *Steinsund*— all cleared their respective ports on the second and third of that month. None was ever heard from again. No trace of the eight ships ever turned up.

Several months previously, the Russian bark *Albyan* and the Spanish steamer *Yute* put to sea from New York and simply vanished without a trace.

It is possible that some of these doomed vessels encountered what was one of the worst winters on record for the North Atlantic. At times, winds had exceeded hurricane force. Hurricane winds in the tropics are dangerous for any vessel. But winds in excess of seventy-five miles an hour, with gusts to ninety knots, roaring down out of the Arctic would be sheer hell. Ships can be coated with ice faster than the crews can hack it away. Eventually, the superstructures and masts are so thickly encased in ice that the ships become top-heavy. The huge seas accompanying the winds could easily capsize such top-heavy vessels if they broached and were caught broadside in a trough between two waves. Useless lifeboats, frozen in place, would have plummeted to the bottom with the ships. They would normally break free from a sinking ship, but now their release levels would be frozen under solid ice. Any survivors would last but a few short minutes, at most, under such disastrous conditions. The waters of the North Atlantic would become as treacherous as those off Cape Horn.

The storms, one on February 6 and the other on February 15, each raged for about seventy-two hours. Never before or since have so many ships disappeared in a small sector of the Atlantic in such a short span of time.

Two years later, the Spanish ship *Mardel Plata*, a coal-carrying freighter, sailed from Scotland on January 30, 1923, for Bilbao, Spain. She was never seen nor heard from again.

Just two weeks later, the 253-foot Dutch cargo ship *Lukkos* sailed from Antwerp for Tangier under the command of a Captain Gieseke. The *Lukkos* was last seen passing the Dungeness headlands off the southeast coast of England. The freighter and her twenty-five-man crew were never seen again.

Less than a year later, on January 3, 1924, the French steamer *Mount Rose*, carrying a cargo of wheat, vanished in the same waters.

A little more than a month after that, on February 8, another French ship, the *Port de Brest*, steamed out of Bordeaux, France, bound for Dakar in West Africa. After being seen off Cape Finisterre, on February 10, she, too, disappeared forever.

The 5,500-ton American freighter *Haleakala* sailed from Norfolk on September 3, 1926, for the River Plate in Uruguay. The last communication from her was received on September 8. Then, she vanished. She may have fallen victim to a great hurricane that ravaged the Caribbean and south Florida with 135-mph winds—but no wreckage from the *Haleakala* was ever found.

A few months later, another American ship, the *John Tracy*, also put to sea from Norfolk. She was carrying a cargo of coal bound for Boston. She was last seen on January 11, off *Pollack Rip* lightship. Nothing is known of her fate after that.

The Italian steamship *Messicano* disappeared shortly after November 23, 1928, while en route to Rotterdam with a cargo of ore.

The Danes are renowned the world over as outstanding mariners, and even today, most Danish naval and merchant cadets receive their training under sail. Two of her square-rigged sailing ships, the *Christian Radich* and the *Danmark*, are known in seaports around the world. But there was another Danish training ship that will be remembered by followers of the sea long after the *Danmark* and *Christian Radich* have made their last port of call.

The *Kobenhavn* was a beautiful square-rigger with one of the most magnificent figureheads ever to part the waters of the seven seas—a carved likeness of the warrier-priest Absalon, who founded the city of Copenhagen. No vessel afloat, under steam or sail, made a better accounting of herself than the *Kobenhavn* during the 1920s.

Her normal complement of officers, two boatswains, a sailmaker, a carpenter, sixteen able-bodied seamen, ten ordinary seamen, and forty-five cadets manned the 375-foot vessel.

Including her bowsprit, her length was 430 feet, and she had a beam of 49 feet. She was a 3,965 gross ton ship. Loaded to the waterline, she drew 24 feet. She was steel-hulled and carried five great steel masts. In addition to her sails—56,000 square feet of them, which weighed over eight tons—she carried an auxiliary diesel engine of 500 horsepower that could propel her along at six knots in fair to smooth seas.

Captain Hans Ferdinand Andersen was the *Kobenhavn*'s master on her tenth transatlantic journey, which was from Denmark to Buenos Aires. All aboard, including the cadets, had previous sea experience under sail. The crossing was uneventful.

On December 14, 1928, she put to sea from Buenos Aires and headed south toward Cape Horn. It was summer in the Southern Hemisphere, and December was the best month to round the Cape. Despite the fact that they were not at home for Christmas, the crew enjoyed the Argentine summer. Their morale was high, for after rounding Cape Horn, the *Kobenhavn* would again be cruising through subtropic seas.

A week into her voyage, the big sailing vessel communicated by radio with the Norwegian steamship *William Blumer*. She was approximately 1100 miles south of Buenos Aires and about to begin her westward beat around the Horn. Captain Andersen reported that all was being well. This was the last that was ever heard from the training ship *Kobenhavn*.

In mid-February, her owners, the East Asiatic Company, became most concerned and two weeks later reported the *Kobenhavn* as being overdue, for nothing had been heard from the ship since she talked to the *William Blumer* in December.

A massive search commenced, probably the most extensive ever conducted in the southern oceans up until then. Every known island where the *Kobenhavn* possibly could have been was searched. Remote bays and estuaries were explored. Even icebergs that were large enough to support survivors were investigated. In fact, every landmark around the earth in the southern latitudes was scoured—but to no avail. The search lasted for over a year.

A court of inquiry was held at the Copenhagen on October 15, 1929. The finding was that the *Kobenhavn* had been struck by an act of God and whatever happened took place so suddenly that there was no time to send out a distress message, let alone launch any life rafts or boats.

Or was there?

Six year later, and half a world away from where the *Kovenhavn* was last heard from, a group of South African fishermen near the Cape of Good Hope were waiting for the weather to settle before launching their boats. As they waited, they searched for firewood. Finding some nearly buried planking, they began scooping the sand away. It was a small boat—a lifeboat! A little more digging, and they uncovered a name on its bow, *Kobenhavn*. They had never heard of the ship, but what they found after further excavation sent them scurrying away in terror. The lifeboat had been manned by a crew of skeletons, survivors of the missing training ship.

Apparently, they had endured whatever it was that happened to the *Kobenhavn*. Although their lifeboat had carried them across the south Atlantic, they had perished from thirst and starvation before the boat was swept onto a South African beach.

Ships continued to disappear right up to and during World War II. The *La Crescenta* steamed out of Port San Luis, near San Luis Obispo, California, on November 24, 1934, bound for Osaka, Japan. Her cargo tanks were filled to capacity. On December 5, the ship radioed the steamer *Athelviscount* that all was well. The *La Cresenta* was never heard from again. No boats, no bodies, no wreckage. Nothing. There was talk that the tanker was overloaded, but no proof of that ever surfaced.

The Western Hemisphere is probably surpassed by the Eastern Hemisphere in its number of vessels that have disappeared without a trace. Every year, a dozen or more ships and fishing craft vanish off the waters around Japan. Far to the south, however, the waters of Australia have probably overwhelmed as many as, if not more than, any other sector of all the seas and oceans in the world. Even before the turn of the last century, strange disappearances at sea were almost commonplace in the waters around Australia and New Zealand—especially in the Tasman Sea, the body of water separating the two countries.

Such was the case of the French motorship *Monique* out of Noumea, New Caledonia. On July 31, 1953, she set out from Maue in the Loyalty Islands for a return trip to Noumea. The 240-ton vessel carried 101 passengers and a crew of 19. Her holds were crammed with general cargo. Her topsides were an obstacle course, for every available space was taken by deck cargo. The *Monique* had been built in 1945 of wood planking over steel frames. Her equipment included a ship-to-shore radio, radar, depth sounder, lifeboats, life rafts, and other emergency gear. Her captain, Charles Ohlen, had made the voyage many times. It was an easy overnight trip that would get the ship back to Noumea the following morning.

That evening, a routine radio message was received from the *Monique*, stating that everything was going well and that she would arrive in Noumea on schedule. Nothing else was ever heard from the French motorship or those aboard her. A 30,000-square-mile search failed to find any trace of the vessel. The weather had been fair both before and after the loss.

Of course, there is also the well publicized *Joyita* mystery mentioned elsewhere in this book. Less well known is the voyage of the *Timaru*, an iron bark that sailed from Lyttleton, New Zealand, on August 16, 1902, bound for Kaipara, New Zealand, with a general cargo. Her skipper, Captain Johnson, had sailed his 120-foot ship through those waters many times. It was routine.

On the morning of August 24, the square-rigger was sighted by the schooner *Morning Light* in the Cook Strait, the body of water that separates North and South Island of New Zealand. Nóthing more was ever seen of the *Timaru* and her eleven-man crew. Within sight of North Island, she simply disappeared.

The three-masted schooner *Toroa* was well known in New Zealand waters during the early years of the twentieth century. The 110-foot vessel was under the command of Captain O. Jarman when she sailed from Greymouth on August 10, 1903, for a coastal voyage to Wanganui on the North Island. Her cargo consisted of 205 tons of coal and five tons of building bricks. However, the bricks were never used for construction, and the coal never burned, for the 164-ton schooner and its seven-man crew were never heard from again.

In Greek mythology, Nemesis is the name of the goddess of vengeance. That was also the name of an Australian tramp steamer that put out to sea from Newcastle, New South Wales, on July 8, 1904, with a cargo of coal destined for Melbourne. Thirty-one persons were aboard the 240-foot ship. Somewhere along the southeast coast of Australia, however, the gods had their vengeance, for the *Nemesis* was never seen or heard from again.

The only trace that was ever found of the *Rio Loge*, an auxiliary brigantine (a sailing vessel with an auxiliary motor for propulsion when not under sail), was a life preserver washed ashore in Wellington Harbor. The ship had sailed from Kaipara, New Zealand, on January 6, 1909, for Dunedin with a cargo of lumber. Twelve men, including her captain, W. S. Spence, were aboard when fate overtook her in the treacherous Cook Strait. The *Rio Loge* had sailed into oblivion.

On September 15, 1911, the coastal steamer *Rosedale* put to sea from Nambucca River for Sydney, New South Wales, Australia. She was last seen at 2:15 P.M. that same day passing Smokey Cape. The *Rosedale* was lost without a trace.

The *Endeavor* was a research vessel belonging to the Australian government working in the desolate waters around Macquarie Island, an area of many vanished ships. The 130-foot ship vanished in 1914 with her crew of twenty-four. An extensive search proved futile.

Many were surprised when the 140-ton schooner *Jubilee* failed to arrive at Nine Island on a voyage from Auckland with a cargo of horses. The ninety-five-foot New Zealand vessel had left Auckland on August 15, 1920, and made one stop at Kawau en route. In addition to the horses, she was carrying seven passengers and a crew of ten when she left Kawau after the two-day layover. When the *Jubilee* put out, the weather was good and everything aboard the schooner intact. She was a well found ship. However, no one knows what happened after the schooner began the final leg of her voyage to Nine Island. No trace, whatsoever, was ever found of her.

A more celebrated disappearance on the sea involves one of the most distinguished racing sailboats of its day. It was a gala occasion when publisher Harvey Conover launched his sleek new yawl *Revonoc* (Conover spelled backwards) at Mamaroneck, New York, in 1956. The event was attended by sailing enthusiasts from all parts of the Northeast, for *Revonoc* was the boat to beat during the upcoming racing season. She was designed for sailing on the open ocean in all weather. Harvey Conover was considered one of the ablest and most experienced "blue water" sailors on the entire eastern seaboard. Few yachtsmen could match him in sailing ability and seamanship.

After a summer of successful racing in her home waters, the *Revonoc* sailed south to Florida, where she took on all comers in the offshore racing circuit. During the week before Christmas, the Conovers enjoyed a relaxing sail down through the Florida Keys.

After spending a joyous Christmas in Key West, Harvey Conover, his wife, daughter, and son-in-law set sail for Miami, 150 miles to the north—a course on which they'd always be in sight of land. Nevertheless, it was still 150 miles through an area that was soon to become known for its lost ships and airplanes—the "Devil's Triangle." Before the Cuban weather stations signed off, which they usually did at dark each night, they gave a marine weather report that forecast good weather.

The *Revonoc* experienced fair sailing until it was off Biscayne Bay just south of Miami. Then, without any warning, an unexpected cold front swooshed in on the yawl. In a few very short minutes, fair sailing breezes were slammed aside by gale force winds from the opposite direction. But Conover was an able sailor, and *Revonoc* was a proven rough weather vessel. Weather like this was nothing new to the man and his boat. And besides, there was to be a gala New Year's celebration at the yacht club that evening.

The year 1957 was blasted out by a howling norther that came roaring down through the Straits of Florida. *Revonoc* plunged onward, for she was only a few short miles from the entrance to Biscayne Bay and refuge from the storm. As the gusting winds exploded across Biscayne Bay, they carried with them the strains of

"Auld Lang Syne," for the Conovers' friends reveling at the club were unaware that one of their sailing buddies and his ship were fighting for their lives just a few miles away.

When the tumultuous first dawn of 1958 broke, *Revonoc* was no more. She had vanished. A search for the missing yacht was immediately undertaken by the coast guard and the navy. As word spread to the Conovers' many friends, they too joined the search—some even risking their own yachts and personal safety. All that was ever found from the *Revonoc* was the yawl's eight-foot dinghy, which washed ashore at Hillsboro Lighthouse, some forty miles north of Miami.

Another yachtsman of world renown was Richard Bertram (Bertram Boats) who participated in the search for *Revonoc* and was a close family friend of the Conovers. Bertram refused to believe that the Conovers had succumbed to the sea and weather. "Harvey Conover was too good a sailor to let that happen to him," said Bertram. He felt that the missing yawl was most likely run down by a ship and ground to pieces by the churning propellers. This is a possibility, for several reasons. A steady stream of southbound ships hug the Florida coastline to avoid the northward push of the Gulf Stream, which is virtually a river within the sea. With the advent of highly sophisticated radar, many vessels, particularly those of foreign registry, began to eliminate a bow lookout. A wooden boat such as *Revonoc*, in a very turbulent sea, would be difficult to detect on a radar screen. A fully loaded ship, such as a tanker, could run down even a large yacht and the ship's crew would not feel it, especially if the ship were rising and falling with large seas. There are numerous documented incidents of ships smashing into small craft and continuing on their way completely oblivious that an accident had taken place. Could this have happened to *Revonoc*? If so, why did her little eight-foot dinghy survive unscathed?

The Christmas season. Yes, it is the season to be jolly, a time of joy and merriment. But it is also the time of the year when most disappearances at sea seem to occur.

It was but two days before Christmas and the first day of winter in 1967, when another yacht emerged in the news. Forty-two-year-old Dan Burack, a Miami Beach hotel owner, and Father Patrick Horgan, thirty-five, a priest from Saint George's Catholic Church in Fort Lauderdale, felt the merriment of the season as they cast off the lines from Burack's twenty-three-foot white, twin-engined Chris Craft cabin cruiser. As the boat worked its way through the labyrinth of canals surrounding Burack's island home in one of Miami Beach's most affluent neighborhoods, they commented on the decorative Christmas lights being turned on along their route to Government Cut and the ocean. They had planned to watch the Christmas lights from a few hundred yards off-shore. It was 8:00 P.M. on Friday, December 22, 1967. A cold front was moving toward Miami from the northwest. However, the concrete walls of the hotels and apartment building and the Miami Beach shoreline provided good protection from the increasing winds.

At 8:30 P.M., they cleared Government Cut, the inlet leading from Miami Harbor to the ocean. Revving both engines to full throttle, the two men headed seaward to behold the Christmas lights of Miami Beach from a half mile out at sea—a half mile that was to stretch into infinity. At 9:00 P.M., the Miami Beach coast guard received a radio message from Burack that his boat had become disabled after the propellers of his outdrives had struck a submerged object. However, he reported that the boat was safe and wasn't taking on water.

At 9:03 P.M. a forty-foot coast guard cutter was on its way to assist. Here were men who knew those waters like the palm of their hands. They were professionals, fully trained in every phase of search and rescue.

Meanwhile, Burack and Father Horgan, knowing that built-in flotation chambers made their boat unsinkable, had little to do but watch the Christmas lights from the vicinity of buoy number 7 off Government Cut. The northwesterly wind had little effect on sea conditions so close to shore.

Unaware that they'd be spending their Christmas searching for a missing boat, the coast guard crew reached the position given by Burack eighteen minutes after receiving his first call. All they found was buoy number 7 marking the ship channel into the harbor. There was no sign of the disabled craft or its occupants.

A search was conducted from the Florida Keys to Jacksonville and 150 miles out to sea. Yet, there was no trace of her.

After being fully cooperative with the press throughout the first five days of the search, the coast guard suddenly refused to release the contents of Burack's only radio message. A coast guard legal officer said they were not at liberty to divulge the information.

Friends of Burack stated that although he was not a "blue water–rough seas" sailor, he was fully capable of handling his boat and had it equipped with every safety device available for a craft of its size.

After the search was called off, a coast guard spokesman said, "We presume they are missing, but not lost at sea." And "missing" they were: Father Patrick Horgan, Dan Burack, and a twenty-three-foot cabin cruiser that lived up to its name—*Witchcraft*!

Could the yacht have been blown seaward by rising winds even as the coast guard was nearing her original position? There was a radio aboard, but perhaps the *Witchcraft* was taking on water and her batteries flooded, putting the radio out of commission. Also, if Burack was as experienced and his boat as well equipped as his friends stated, why didn't he just anchor? His original position was in water varying from thirty to forty feet in depth. Furthermore, the boat was "unsinkable."

And what about the coast guard spokesman who, five days into the search, suddenly refused to comment on Burack's distress message other than to say that he sounded as though he was in an "unusual" situation? Burack's last words, or at least the last ones that the coast guard released, were, "It's pretty odd. I've never seen one like this!"

At 2:30 on the afternoon of June 19, 1972, a 1964 white Chevrolet Impala convertible pulled off Sunrise Boulevard, one of Fort Lauderdale's main thoroughfares, into a parking space on Highway A1A, which runs parallel to the ocean. The top was down, and sticking up out of the backseat was an eight-foot sailing dinghy. Seventeen-year-old Tom Robinson of Fort Lauderdale was taking his girlfriend, Cathy Wheeler, also seventeen, for an afternoon sail. They left their billfolds, shoes, Cathy's glasses, and other personal things locked in the trunk. The two teenagers, dressed in T-shirts and cut-off blue jeans, lugged the red and white boat down to the water's edge.

Fort Lauderdale is known for having one of the safest beaches in southeast Florida. For three miles, there is no concrete wall of hotels and high-rise apartment buildings obstructing public access to the beach, as is so common along the other beaches of Florida's Atlantic and Gulf coasts. There is little undertow to endanger swimmers during the summer months. Large waves, to the dismay of surfers, are rare, except during inclement weather. The Bahama Islands, fifty miles to the east, form a natural barrier against the long Atlantic swells. The rare shark encounters have been nips and nonfatal bites rather than deadly strikes. Potentially, the most dangerous aspect of this beach is pollution caused by outfall of sewage, originating from Miami Beach and Hollywood to the south, being carried north by the outer fringes of the Gulf Stream.

As Tom and Cathy shoved off from shore, they must have been the envy of those who had to be content with lying in the warm sand or frolicking in the gentle surf at one of the most crowded sections of Fort Lauderdale's beach. Tom and Cathy had just graduated from Stranahan High School, and both had been accepted for college in the fall. They were young and had the whole world before them.

It was 3:00 P.M. when they stepped the mast, raised the small boat's sail, and wove their way between dozens of bathers relaxing in the clear warm water. Their plans were to stay within a few hundred feet from shore, tacking the boat parallel to the beach. A gentle wind was blowing from the west. Only a few scattered clouds blemished the sky. The sun was still high above

Schrafft's Hotel across the street. They were seen laughing and having a good time less than a hundred yards from the beach. That was the last that was ever seen of Catherine Ann Wheeler, honor student, and Thomas Robinson, high school football star, and their little red and white sailboat. All that remained was the 1964 white Chevrolet Impala convertible, alone, still parked after all the other vehicles had left for the day.

The next morning a search and rescue operation commenced, or rather was expanded—for this made three boats that the coast guard was looking for. Eighteen-year-old Steven Whithurst of West Palm Beach was missing in his eighteen-foot motorboat, *Doc's Order*. Also missing was a thirty-five-foot sailboat carrying six young men, a girl, and a dog. The latter was poorly rigged and carried no name or numbers, and the crew was completely unfamiliar with even the basic fundamentals of sailing. They were last seen struggling through trial and error to raise the sails as the boat was moving north in the Gulf Stream—sideways.

Two days later, the Greek ship *Delphic Eagle* found young Steven Whithurst adrift 140 miles east off St. Augustine—over 400 miles from where he was last seen, but still safe and sound.

The following day, the thirty-five-foot sailboat with its neophyte crew was found tied to an abandoned dock not far from where the attempted cruise had originated.

But Tom Robinson and Cathy Wheeler were still missing. The coast guard searched an area larger than Vermont, Rhode Island, and New Hampshire combined. Lieutenant D. C. Hibbard and Lieutenant Commander H. C. McKean had just returned from a ten-hour search mission covering over fourteen hundred square miles in the area between and to the north of Palm Beach and Grand Bahama Island. They were relaxing at the base officers' club. As Hibbard poured a beer into his glass, he commented, "There are two kids out there, and we haven't found them. We've searched every inch of that water. And when you can't find those kids, and you know they're in a tight situation, it really gets to you."

At dawn the next day, the two officers and their crew of six were aloft again, searching a different grid section in their Albatross amphibian. They were flying at 750 feet with a cruising speed of 125 miles per hour. Two observers, secured by safety belts, were leaning out the back door. They would alternately observe for one hour and be relieved for one hour with another pair of observers. Thus, the pilot, copilot, and two observers were continuously scanning the waters beneath the plane as were the crews of five other planes, three helicopters, and a number of surface vessels. The waters were clear and calm. The search lasted for days, but no trace of the little white and red boat or its two young occupants was ever found.

For decades and longer, seafarers and maritime writers have maintained that the sea is unforgiving. Swallowing up vessels from dinghies to dreadnaughts, it is also very nondiscriminatory.

The stories of missing ships and yachts, vessels that just sailed off over the horizon and were never seen or heard from again, can go on and on. Most became repetitious from what little is known about them. They are simply missing or lost without a trace.

THREE

The *Queen*'s Phantom Guests

T he *Queen Mary*'s four screws, driven by 200,000 horsepower engines, hacked through a defiant surge as they pushed 81,000 tons of supreme luxury into the ruthless seas off Cape Horn. She was the undisputed queen of the oceans, on her final voyage.

Her decks had once been paced by the Marx Brothers, Douglas Fairbanks, Jr., Clark Gable, Charles Lindberg, Amelia Earhart, Charlie Chaplin, Ginger Rogers, Mary Pickford, Joan Crawford, Jean Harlow, Laurel and Hardy, the Rockefellers, Winston Churchill, and almost anyone else who was anybody during the mid-1930s and the post-war years. With the commencement of World War II, the ship went to war, her decks tread by an army of fighting men including Colonel James Stewart. West-bound, she hauled thousands of German prisoners of war to Canada and the United States.

Now, on the last voyage, her passenger list consisted of myriad high rollers from both sides of the Atlantic who craved to be part of the *Queen Mary*'s final sea journey. Her crew, many the pick of the Cunard Line's senior employees, fulfilled their responsibilities in an atmosphere of nostalgia, for an aura of sentiment surrounded the great ship.

However, aboard the majestic liner there were others journeying on that last voyage. They weren't passengers, nor were they part of the crew. Their names didn't appear on the vessel's manifest. But they were there—aboard as they had been for years. For they were the ghosts of the *Queen Mary*.

The *Queen Mary*'s majestic dining saloons became mess halls serving shifts of 2,000 troops at a time. Her cocktail bars, lavish cabins, and staterooms were converted to berthing areas with at least twelve men crowded into each compartment. Every available space aboard the ship was tiered with bunks. And the human capacity of the lower class, or steerage, spaces had been augmented manyfold. Even the swimming pools were boarded over and filled with tiers of bunks, six high. She was converted to carry 16,000 soldiers, or the equivalent of an entire division, on a single voyage. She carried lifeboats for only half that many. Like her Cunarder forbearer, the *Titanic*, "she would never have the need for any more lifeboats."

It was during one of her wartime voyages that the *Queen* experienced the most disquieting episode of her celebrated seagoing career. It did not occur on a fog-shrouded ocean, nor in a storm-pitched sea. No enemy action provoked the tragedy. It wasn't even during the darkness of night. It just happened—one of those things. In fact, the disaster was cloaked in secrecy until after the war.

•   •   •

It was midafternoon on October 2, 1942. The sea was choppy but not excessively rough. The *Queen Mary* had just zigzagged across the Atlantic and was on the home stretch, rounding north of Ireland with 10,000 American soldiers bound for the Clyde River, where the GIs were to disembark. She had been unescorted. It was presumed that her speed and constant course changes made her an extremely difficult target for marauding U-boats. She was the prime target—for Hitler had offered $250,000 and the Iron Cross to the submarine commander who could sink her.

That morning she was joined by an escort, the cruiser HMS *Curacoa* and six destroyers. The *Queen* was now within reach of the Luftwaffe and needed the antiaircraft protection of the other ships. As the distance to land decreased, the sea room became less conducive to zig-zagging.

Lunch aboard the *Curacoa* was over, and the cooks were starting to prepare the evening meal. Most of the off-watch crew were below in their hammocks. Captain John Boutwood, D.S.O., was on the light cruiser's bridge. He was the senior officer in command of the escort ships. He ordered the destroyers to patrol ahead of the *Queen Mary* to shield her from mines and U-boats. Boutwood intended to take position astern of his charge as protection against any possible air strike. The day was clear, with perfect visibility on the open ocean. All eight ships were ready to take immediate protective action in case of an attack. The 4200-ton *Curacoa* and her destroyers had provided similar protection to the liner three times in the past. The 456-foot ship, with her main weaponry of eight 4-inch guns, was designed to fend off and destroy attacking aircraft.

The *Queen Mary* continued her irregular evasive tactics. The six escorting destroyers, under order to yield to the maneuvers of their ward, took their stations ahead. Boutwood, also ahead of the liner, was readying his ship to fall astern.

On the *Queen*'s bridge, her master, Captain Cyril Illingworth, glanced at the bridge clock. It was 1410. All vessels were under a radio-silence directive from the Admiralty. The *Queen* continued her evasive zigzags as before. It was the responsibility of the escorts to keep clear.

Senior First Officer Noel Robinson on the *Queen Mary*'s bridge advised Captain Illingworth that the *Curacoa*, working her way toward the liner's stern, could be close to a converging course. The *Queen*'s helmsman was ordered to put the wheel over several degrees to the port. Almost simultaneously aboard the cruiser, Captain Boutwood, realizing the same situation, ordered his ship to take a starboard tack.

Both vessels were doing almost thirty knots. Their merging bow wakes were creating a tremendous wave. As the ships nearly converged, the turbulence of their combined wash caused each vessel to yaw ever so slightly, effecting a small, barely discernible counter course change for both ships.

Deep down in the liner's engine and fire rooms, the men running the ship felt a slight jar, as if the *Queen* had struck a slightly larger wave. On the bridge Captain Illingworth, who was taking a quick glance at a chart, felt the insignificant bump. Whatever it was, he thought, it had evidently left his ship unscathed.

The resulting minor course changes effected by the rampage of the ships' wakes had caused the liner to nudge the *Curacoa*'s stern. The glancing impact, combined with the ships' own turbulent wash, was enough to throw the cruiser out of control and cause her to careen off course, ending up broadside directly in the path of the *Queen Mary*'s enormous bow.

Aboard the cruiser, a terrified Captain Boutwood looked up to his port. Before he or anyone else could react, the *Queen Mary*'s massive prow cleaved into the *Curacoa* amidship. Those in the warship's engine room and other belowdeck spaces had but a fleeting glance of the troopship's stem ripping through the hull of their ship before they were inundated by thousands of tons of seawater. The *Queen Mary* smashed on through the *Curacoa* like a fire axe through a beer can. There was no slowing down, no rescue attempt, and no distress calls. She had been under direct Admiralty orders to stop or slow down under no circumstances whatsoever. Captain Illingworth had no choice but to maintain his ship's speed, tearing the hapless cruiser in two.

The forward half of the *Curacoa*, still under momentum, glided along the *Queen Mary*'s port side. The stern section, her engines stopped when the seawater flooded her stokeholds, wafted aimlessly along the liner's starboard beam. Within minutes both sections of the cruiser plunged down into the frigid depths. Of the *Curacoa*'s 439 officers and men, 338 perished in the sea.

The *Queen Mary* suffered only minor damage, none of which required immediate repairs. There were no casualties aboard the liner. Thus, after offloading her troops, she was able to sail back to the United States for repairs.

The *Queen Mary* served throughout the rest of the war unscathed. After the surrender of Germany, she was used for carrying American troops home from the European Theater. In addition, she transported at least twenty thousand GI war brides to the United States. She also carried a number of Canadian war brides to Halifax. And the welcomes she experienced at each arrival in New York were greater than any festivity during her earlier peacetime arrivals.

The *Queen Mary* operated under United States authority for more than a year after the war's end before returning to the John Brown Shipyard in Southampton for conversion back to a luxury liner. It took thirty tons of paint in Cunard colors to replace the *Queen*'s scraped-off camouflage.

Her post-war service was uneventful. At first, she and her sister ship, the *Queen Elizabeth*, were the preference of the rich and famous, and the not so rich and famous, for transatlantic transportation. But by the mid-1960s, the handwriting was on the wall for both vessels. It was not old age or newer, more modern ships—it was the jet age. Lower transatlantic airfares and overnight flights were doing the luxury ships in.

In October 1967, the *Queen Mary* steamed down the English Channel for the last time. The final voyage was to Long Beach, California, via Cape Horn (she was too large for the Panama Canal). She carried 1200 paying passengers. The journey lasted thirty-nine days. Rounding the tip of South America, the *Queen Mary* encountered some of the roughest water in her thirty years at sea. The waves, often referred to as "grey beards," were as high as forty feet and, being far apart, were rougher for the liner than they may have been for a smaller vessel. But, like the good ship she was, the *Queen* made it around the Horn and up the west coast of South America with nothing more catastrophic than a lot of upset stomachs.

The city of Long Beach had purchased the *Queen Mary* for $3,400,000. As the giant liner reached her destination, thousands of red and white carnations were dropped on her from welcoming aircraft. She was to be permanently docked as a floating hotel, convention center, museum, and restaurant. The cost of conversion from ocean liner to tourist attraction skyrocketed another fifty million dollars. It was during the transformation to a civic facility that things—strange things—began to happen aboard the ship that had made 1,001 transatlantic crossings.

The *Queen Mary* was a large ship, a floating city, never putting out to sea with less than a thousand people aboard and sometimes with more than 16,000, plus the crew. And with so many people aboard, accidents and mishaps were bound to happen. One incident had occurred on July 10, 1966, when John Pedder, an eighteen-year-old engine room worker, was crushed to death when an automatic door closed on him. It was doorway number thirteen. The ship's first captain, Sir Edgar Britten, died only weeks after the liner's maiden voyage.

During the *Queen's* days as a troopship, a fracas broke out in one of the ship's galleys. The brawl became serious enough that the captain had to radio a nearby cruiser to send a boarding crew to break up the near mutiny. Before the escorting ship's squad arrived, a ship's cook was shoved into a hot oven and later died of his burns.

An officer died during his watch on the vessel's bridge. The cause of death was attributed to food poisoning. During that same time period, a young woman drowned in the ship's swimming pool. There had been incidents of passengers having fallen overboard.

During the *Queen Mary*'s thirty-one years at sea, except for her collision with the HMS *Curacoa*, it is likely that for a vessel of the *Queen*'s size and the number of persons who were carried aboard, the number of accidents and fatalities was less than would be expected.

Strange things, however, began to happen aboard the *Queen Mary* during her conversion at Long Beach. Workers, especially those laboring deep in the bowels of the ship, complained of tools disappearing and then showing up later, exactly where they originally had been left.

Carol Zalfini, a secretary, was passing an engine room entrance one evening after the workers had left for the day when she heard pounding and clanging from below. Thinking some of the workers had remained on overtime, she went below to where she thought the sounds had originated. She found herself alone in silence. When she climbed back toward the upper level, the sounds commenced once again. As she started back down, the noise stopped. This is when she fled the engine room. When she mentioned the incident to others, they scoffed at her.

A short time later, Security Sergeant Nancy Wazny was standing next to a stairway leading to the swimming pool. No outsiders were supposed to be in that part of the ship at the time. The pool had been drained, but there, next to the pool, Wazny saw a middle-aged woman in a one-piece bathing suit. She appeared to be from the 1950s or earlier, and she looked ready to dive into the empty pool. "When I screamed at her, she disappeared." According to the ship's records, a woman passenger had once drowned in the pool.

Robert Shuster of the *Los Angeles Daily News* wrote, "One night, a security guard patrolling the ship with a specially trained dog heard a noise behind watertight door No. 13. The dog suddenly stopped, or so the story goes, refusing to move any further. A search of the area turned up nothing, but archive records show that it is the same door that fatally crushed young John Pedder on July 10, 1966.

"Years after the security guard incident, a tour guide, walking up some steps aboard the ship, felt the presence of a stranger behind her. She quickly turned and saw the image of a young man for a brief second, before the apparition disappeared. The guide, who didn't know about the violent death in doorway No. 13, later picked Pedder's picture from a lineup of several others.

" 'I was there when she did it, and my heart went to my throat,' said Jennnifer Nestegard, a publicist for the *Queen Mary*. 'It was really frightening.' "

The *Queen Mary*'s security lieutenant, Fred McMullin, tells of incidents where doors and hatches that had been secured and locked mysteriously opened during the hours just after midnight. Some were even propped open. The doors and hatches were locked and double-checked by numerous people. However, according to McMullin, "we'd go on our rounds. And, son of a gun, we would find them open again."

Tom Hennessy of the *Miami Herald* told of how he was given permission to spend a night aboard the *Queen*. "I looked at my watch. It was 2:15 A.M. I was walking along the shaft alley (the compartments in the bottom of the ship where the shafts connecting the engines to the propeller are located), and it was about as much fun as a coffin. Suddenly I heard some loud clanging noise like the sound of someone banging on pipes. I walked toward the noise. You have only my word for what followed, but as I neared the source, the noise stopped. As I retreated, it resumed.

"Moments later, I was walking the passageway leading from the shaft alley. I had just come through this passageway, and it had been clear. Now it was partly blocked by an oil drum. I returned to the shaft alley. I am not a skittish person. The only spirits to which I pay homage are distilled. When I turned and reentered the passageway, I found it blocked by two oil drums."

After working his way past the drums, Hennessy walked along a catwalk. "It seemed to be vibrating as if someone was walking toward me. Then there was a sudden rush of wind in an area that was supposed to be airtight. I changed directions faster than Herschel Walker.

"Then at 3:33 A.M., I heard the worst. Initially, it sounded like two or three men talking at once. But it trailed off to a single voice, so distinct that I made out the end of a sentence: 'turning the lights off.'

"Back up near the pool, I found a narrow, dark passageway with a dozen dressing rooms on each side, rooms, to my knowledge, that haven't been used in more than a decade. In four of the rooms, the lights came on. I did not investigate. Mrs. Hennessy may have raised a coward, but not a fool."

There have been reports of Sir Edgar Britten, the *Queen*'s first captain, who died aboard the ship, being seen pacing the ship's bridge.

Kathy Lowe, a supervisor, was standing by the empty swimming pool one day. She watched in shock as wet footprints mysteriously materialized one by one along the pool deck. The pool was empty.

Workers in the engine rooms have reported seeing a strange man in blue coveralls lurking among steam pipes leading to the ship's engines. He would simply vanish when approached. Ghostly apparition or workers' resourceful imaginations?

The most often reported eerie happening on the *Queen Mary* is the most shocking. John L. Smith, a marine engineer aboard the ship, first experienced it when the liner was approaching the California coast. "I first heard men screaming while the old ship was still at sea. I was below deck at the bow, as far forward as anyone could get when it happened. It was the voices of horrified men screaming in panic and followed by the terrible noise of crunching metal being ripped apart and the rush of water. It was coming from outside the bow where there was only the sea."

After the vessel was permanently berthed, the dreadful clamor of two ships in collision periodically horrified others aboard the *Queen Mary*. The raging pandemonium of shrieks and grinding steel always seemed to emanate from outside the ship's bow. Could it be that the *Curacoa* and her unearthly crew have been doomed to an eternity of reliving that terrible October afternoon in 1942?

As word reached the general public about the bizarre events aboard the old luxury liner, thousands of curious sightseers, tourists and locals alike, have clambered to see for themselves. There have been so many, in fact, that official "ghost" tours are now conducted aboard the old *Queen Mary*.

Some skeptical readers will feel that what you have

just read is all hogwash. If you are one of them, my advice to you is to visit the *Queen Mary*. Better, yet, why not ask for permission to spend a night alone aboard the ship near watertight door No. 13—or, maybe, in one of the lower compartments at the bow?

FOUR

The Jinxed Battleship

Probably the *Great Eastern*, a huge ship built in the mid-1800s, is the best known of all ships to carry a jinx. From the day her massive keel was put down in 1854 to the day in 1890 when ship breakers dismantling her found a human skeleton between the vessel's three-foot-high double bottoms—apparently that of a workman accidentally sealed in the compartment during construction forty-four years earlier, the *Great Eastern*'s career was spanned with accidental deaths and mishaps of all descriptions. During the twentieth century, however, an even larger vessel suffered an even more appalling fate during her short life. And it served the most unlikely service, the German Navy in World War II. Her designers said the ship was to be second to no other warship in the world when her keel was laid down in 1935.

The *Scharnhorst* had a tonnage in excess of 32,000. She was equipped with the latest electronic equipment of the period. Her superrange eleven-inch guns, com-

45

bined with her speed, made her potentially the most formidable warship afloat, the battleship of all battleships.

The *Scharnhorst* would normally have been the ship every man in the navy would long to serve on. But the *Scharnhorst* was not a normal ship. Very few volunteered to serve aboard her. The majority of the crew had to be drafted from other ships of the German Navy. Yet there was a waiting list for those who wanted to serve aboard her sister ship, the *Gneisenau*. The *Scharnhorst*, according to hearsay throughout the fleet, was a jinxed ship.

While the big warship sat on the ways during construction, some supports gave way, and the *Scharnhorst* rolled onto her side. Sixty-one workmen were crushed beyond recognition. Another 110 were seriously injured. The ship was righted, and the work went on.

As the day of launching approached, it was announced that the three highest Nazi leaders, Hitler, Goering, and Goebbels, would attend the ceremony, but they were destined never to see the launching of their navy's most promising ship. At some time during the early morning hours on the day of the launching, the huge steel cables holding the ship on the ways parted, and with only a few yard workers and watchmen as spectators, a prelaunch launching took place. As the huge *Scharnhorst* slid into the water, uncontrolled, she rammed directly into two docked destroyers, severely damaging them.

The *Scharnhorst*'s first combat action was in the bombardment of the city of Danzig. Newsreel films, released to the world by the German government, showed the rapid firepower of the ship's weaponry during the attack. These films, seen in theaters on both sides of the Atlantic, also showed the destruction inflicted by the ship's big guns. But what they didn't show was that the *Scharnhorst* was a jinxed ship.

During the bombardment of Danzig, nine of the *Scharnhorst*'s crewmen were killed when one of the turrets exploded during the raid. When an air exhaust ventilator in another turret failed, twelve men suffered an agonizing death. These two accidents were not due to enemy action; the *Scharnhorst* received no hits whatsoever during the barrage. The bombardment of the civilian-occupied city was the greatest victory of the German ship's war record.

During her short-lived career, the *Scharnhorst* took part in several engagements against units of the Royal Navy. Although she did not actually sink any enemy vessels by herself, she did assist the *Gneisenau* in sinking a number of lightly armed Allied merchant ships and the British aircraft carrier *Glorious*. A British destroyer, the *Acasta*—also sunk in this action—managed to get off a single torpedo before going down. It struck the *Scharnhorst*, doing only minor damage due to her 40-inch armor belt.

After the engagement with British warships off the Norwegian coast, the Germans fled the scene. Had they not steamed south back to their base, and instead continued their patrol, they would have encountered a merchant ship and a cruiser carrying the King of Norway to England, an opportunity that could have changed the *Scharnhorst*'s blemished history to one of renown. But, the *Scharnhorst* continued her withdrawal, and as she was about to enter the Elbe River, her radar failed, causing her to ram into the liner *Bremen* anchored at the mouth of the river. The *Bremen*, desperately needed to transport troops, had to be removed from service for months.

When the *Scharnhorst* put to sea again, she received word that a large Allied merchant convoy was headed in her direction. As contact was established with the convoy on Christmas Day, 1943, the German ship discovered that a squadron of Allied warships was trailing the merchant vessels. They included the battleship *Duke of York*, some cruisers, and a number of destroyers. At 4:30 P.M., shortly after the engagement commenced, one of the fourteen-inch guns of the British battleship scored a direct hit just below the *Scharnhorst*'s waterline, penetrating the armor belt. There, in complete darkness, five hundred miles north of the Arctic Circle with seas running high under strong winds, the ships slugged it out. The German ship was losing speed. The *Duke of York* kept hammering away at the German with her fourteen-inch guns. The German return fire caused only minor damage to the *Duke of York*.

The *Scharnhorst*, her engine rooms flooding, stopped dead in the water. A squadron of torpedo-laden Allied destroyers moved in for the kill. At 6:00 P.M., the *Scharnhorst*'s big guns went silent. Her secondary armament continued firing wildly as the torpedos streaked her way.

At 7:00 P.M., her commander, Admiral Bey, sent the ship's final communication, addressed to Hitler and the German Admiralty, "Long live Germany and the Fuehrer!" At 7:28 the *Duke of York* fired the last of her seventy-seven salvos at the *Scharnhorst*. Fifty-two torpedos had already torn into the *Scharnhorst*'s hull, and at 7:37 the destroyer HMS *Jamaica* hit her with three more from a distance of less than two miles.

At 7:45 P.M., the pride of Hitler's navy exploded in a

mushroom of flames and slid beneath the waves at a point northeast of North Cape, Norway. Of the nearly two thousand crewmen aboard the *Scharnhorst*, only thirty-eight survived. All but two of those were taken prisoner.

Two survivors, who managed to escape capture, somehow made it to the Norwegian coast. However, that was not far enough away to elude the jinx of the *Scharnhorst*. After reaching shore, the two prepared a makeshift shelter and started to light an emergency gasoline stove that they had taken from the *Scharnhorst*. There was a flash of flame—an explosion. Gas leaking from the stove had caught fire, mortally burning both of them.

FIVE

Cyclops

J ust like her namesake, the mythical lumbering one-eyed giant, the USS *Cyclops* was ruled by one eye and one eye only, that of Lieutenant Commander George W. Worley. This twentieth-century Captain Bligh paced back and forth the length of the flying bridge, carrying a cane, wearing a derby hat, dressed in long underwear, and savagely chewing the end of a cigar. Had Jack London ever met him, it would have been George Worley and not Wolf Larson in command of the schooner *Ghost* in London's literary classic *The Sea Wolf*.

Silhouetted against the glare of a full moon, one might have mistaken Worley for a gorilla. And looks were not deceiving, for he possessed the strength of three men, as his crew had found out on more than one occasion. Every movement of muscle, from the sway of his shoulders to his lips twisting around the cigar, was in unison with the heave of the *Cyclops* as she steamed south from Norfolk, Virginia, with a cargo of coal, mail, and supplies destined for a fleet of United States warships stationed off the east coast of South America in January 1918.

The huge 19,000-ton coaling ship, her hull pressed low in the water by the bulk of her cargo, rolled sluggishly as she departed the frigid waters of the North Atlantic and plied southward through the warm, tropical waters of the northward-flowing Gulf Stream. The ship's skeletal frameworks of gantries, booms, and other coal-handling apparatus, along with her twin side-by-side stacks, gave her the appearance of some enormous pre-historic creature that had awakened from eons of sleep.

Her crew—those not on watch or sacked out in their bunks below—lined the rail at the ship's bow, mystified by the effect of the prow slicing through the phospho-rescent sea.

At times, one or another of the men cast an uneasy glance at the shadow pacing the flying bridge. Those who had sailed with Worley before knew that this could, with a sudden mood swing from the captain, become a "hell ship." However, no one knew, neither crewmen nor their master, that the *Cyclops* had already began one of the most disastrous voyages in the chronicles of the United States Navy.

The crew, both officers and men, dared not stand up to this walking hurricane of a captain. But like the bar-racuda, forever ferreting a coral reef for its prey, Worley, too, had to have a victim. This voyage it was a young officer, Ensign Cain, who as a result of the captain's harassment was placed in the sick bay by Dr. Burt J. Asper, the ship's surgeon, to prevent his becoming com-pletely demented. Yet there was one man aboard the collier who would face down the commanding officer. He was Lieutenant Harvey Forbes, the executive officer.

But he, too, would eventually fall before the wrath of the *Cyclops*'s master.

"Sometimes I thought Captain Worley was born fifty years or even a century too late. He was a perfect example of the tyrannical "bucko" sailing-ship master[s] who considered their crews not as human beings but merely as a means of getting their vessels to the next port. He was a gruff eccentric salt of the old school, given to carrying a cane but possessing few other qualities. He was a very indifferent seaman and a poor, overly cautious navigator . . . unfriendly and taciturn, generally disliked by both his officers and his men." These were the words of Conrad Nervig, who—as a navy ensign in 1918—was the last crew member to sign off the *Cyclops* before she sailed off into nothingness.

"I first met Captain Worley in November of 1917, when I reported aboard the *Cyclops*. He seemed a nice gentleman. It was only later that I discovered his peculiarities. He would visit me on the bridge during my dog watch [midnight to 4:00 A.M.] carrying a cane, dressed in long underwear, and wearing a derby hat. He would lean on the bridge rail looking at the sea ahead and talking of his family and child, but was quite erratic at times. Without the slightest pause between words, his mood would change to that of a very opinionated man—a self-proclaimed genius who thought he had never arrived but should have. It was while in these moods that he would take out his rage on some unknowing officer. Although he treated me very well. He seemed to like me. Why? I don't know. It was part of his makeup. When it came time for me to leave the ship, he tried to get the admiral of the South Atlantic Patrol Fleet to have me stay. Fortunately I got away, or I wouldn't be here now."

And how right Nervig was, for had Worley been able to keep him aboard the *Cyclops*, there would have been no one at hand fifty-two years later when Nervig stood before a camera, telling about his life aboard the big navy coaling ship for the documentary film *The Devil's Triangle*.

Nervig recalled the mood of the ship. "One of the bad features aboard that ship was the gloom in the wardroom. It was such a depressing place due to the strange behavior of the captain. Everyone was unhappy. It was a relief to take my watch on the bridge with nothing but the moonlight and the nice balmy weather. It was a great sedative after the depression below."

Captain Worley brought the black-and-white camouflaged ship that he had commanded since it was launched in 1910 through the Caribbean and into the South Atlantic. But it was a voyage not without incident. "So many unusual things happened to the *Cyclops* on her trip to South America," Nervig went on. "First, in leaving the Norfolk Navy Yard, she almost had a collision with the USS *Survey* outward bound for antisubmarine duty in the Mediterranean; the head blew off one of the main engines. This meant we had to finish the trip on one engine; she sailed past the port of Rio, our destination, and only daylight saved her from going up on the rocks. Then there was the poor seaman who was drowned after being hit by one of the ship's propellers. Then, after coaling the cruiser *Raleigh*, she scraped the side of that ship, causing some damage."

Completely oblivious to the lights and camera crew, Nervig continued as if he had been physically conveyed back in time. (This interview was conducted in 1970.) "All of this I attribute to Worley's poor navigation and his poor seamanship. Our close call with the rocks off Rio was a perfect example. Lieutenant Forbes had already plotted our course for that port. The captain made some changes, which resulted in our near catastrophe. When Forbes confronted Worley about why he had changed his original course and nearly wrecked the ship, Worley exploded and had Forbes immediately placed under arrest and confined to quarters." But this time the *Cyclops* reached her destination, Rio de Janeiro.

A month earlier, when Nervig first reported aboard the *Cyclops* on November 21, 1917, an incident occurred aboard the USS *Pittsburgh* while anchored in the harbor at Rio that possibly precipitated the fate of the *Cyclops*.

The *Pittsburgh*, the flagship of the South American Patrol Fleet, was under the command of Captain George B. Bradshaw. Before reporting to station off the east coast of South America, the *Pittsburgh* had served with the navy's Pacific Fleet based in San Francisco. She was there when the United States entered World War I. For one reason or another, a number of San Francisco street toughs had joined the navy and were assigned to Captain Bradshaw's ship. They were quite clannish and formed the nucleus of an undesirable element aboard the cruiser, a common situation when large groups of men are brought together under conditions of stress. Most were assigned below deck in the engine and fire rooms, where they bullied most of their shipmates, including some of the petty officers.

On the same date that Ensign Nervig joined the *Cyclops* in Norfolk, a number of the San Francisco gang were gathered in one of the *Pittsburgh*'s boiler rooms. Most of the ship's crew had gone ashore on liberty, but the San Franciscans either elected to stay aboard or were restricted to the ship for disciplinary reasons. A petty officer and an on-duty fireman were also in the fire room, maintaining the fire in boiler number six. Shortly after 11:00 P.M., the group was joined by Fireman First Class James Coker and Fireman Second Class Barney DeVoe who brought a few bottles of liquor. It wasn't long before tempers and inhibitions were near an end.

Homosexuality was a problem in the "old" navy. Although not prevalent, it did exist. Among the group was a young Texan, Fireman Third Class Oscar Stewart, who—although not actually accepted by the "gang,"—was tolerated by them, probably because he often responded favorably to homosexual advances in exchange for candy and other favors. For years afterward, through World War II and beyond, navy old-timers joked about candy bars as "pogey bait." Several weeks previously Coker and DeVoe had made advances to Stewart, who rejected them with the excuse that he had contacted gonorrhea from a girl he had met. He explained that he hadn't reported to the sick bay for fear of being disciplined, and he didn't have enough money to seek medical attention ashore. Coker and DeVoe dug into their pockets and came up with enough money to get treatment from a doctor in Rio de Janeiro. Stewart, for some reason, hadn't seen his two shipmates again until the night of the party in fireroom number six.

Petty Officer Moss Whiteside was in charge of the watch and actually took part in the drinking. At midnight, Whiteside was relieved by Petty Officer John Morefield, who, although he did not participate in the party, did nothing to stop it—probably out of fear. As the night advanced, most of the celebrants staggered off to their quarters. Among those who remained were DeVoe, Coker, and Stewart. Drunkenly working their way over to where Stewart was sitting, Coker and DeVoe propositioned the tipsy Texan. Then the trio moved into a nearby empty coal bunker.

As the story goes, Stewart submitted to his shipmates' advances and, after the act was over, slurred, "That money you all gave me for the doctor, well, on the way to see him, I met these two whores. Now," he said, laughing aloud, "they got what I got, and so have you all."

Before the echo of Stewart's laughter settled, the two others were on him with flying fists. Morefield, the only sober man left, broke up the fight and then left to go about his duties. All was quiet except for the roar of the boiler and the hiss of steam. When Morefield went up to the second level to check on a leaking pump, Coker and DeVoe dragged the unconscious Stewart behind one of the boilers. Fearing that their victim might spread the word about their homosexual act and the venereal disease, Coker beat the Texan about the head with a hammer while DeVoe stood lookout. By the time Morefield returned to the lower level, the two culprits had hidden their victim and sneaked out of the fireroom via an emergency exit. Their plan was to return later, cut the Texan into pieces small enough to fit into the firebox under the boiler, and let the flames dispose of the body.

During the next watch, however, a messenger passing through the fireroom heard moans from somewhere under the catwalk he was crossing. Upon investigation, he discovered Stewart slumped behind the boiler with his bloodied head shattered open. Realizing that the injured crewman was still alive, the messenger went for help.

Stewart was taken to the *Pittsburgh*'s sick bay, where he remained unconscious. Learning that their victim had been found alive, the two assailants decided that they had better get going while the getting was good. Pocketing a collection of money coerced from various individuals and other members of the gang, Coker and DeVoe jumped ship in style—they stole the captain's gig and sailed to Portugal. Their freedom, however, was short-lived. Rumors of two strangers who didn't speak Portuguese brought authorities storming into their mountainside hideout.

Stewart lingered on for nearly a month without ever regaining consciousness. With his death, murder charges were brought against Coker and DeVoe, and they were placed in the ship's brig. Double security was ordered because of the risk that other gang members might attempt to free them. Petty Officers Whiteside and Morefield were also placed under arrest. Whiteside was charged with failing to stop and participating in a drunken party. Morefield was confined for not reporting a drunken party.

The court-martial convened the day before Christmas. Coker was found guilty of murder and sentenced to death by hanging. DeVoe was sentenced to fifty to ninety years in prison for his complicity in the murder. Whiteside received a fifteen-year sentence for not reporting or stopping a drunken party, participating in a drunken party, and perjury. Morefield, who was not a member of the gang, had an unblemished service record, and had already been recommended for promotion, was given five years for not stopping a drunken party. All but Coker were to be transported to the Naval Prison at

Portsmouth, New Hampshire, "by the first available transportation."

A month later, on January 28, the *Cyclops* arrived in Rio. The following day Worley reported to the flagship for orders. His instructions were to receive five court-martialed prisoners. In addition to those involved in Stewart's murder, there were two marine privates named Stamey and Hill, each sentenced to two years for being AWOL. Worley's reaction to the situation is unknown. The only things that the prisoners knew about the *Cyclops* before they boarded her was that "the brig at Portsmouth wouldn't be as bad as Worley's ship."

On Sunday, February 3, the *Pittsburgh* was preparing to put to sea. Forty-two men from the cruiser, who were being sent back to the United States for reassignment, were transferred to the *Cyclops* as passengers. A number of the transferees had been friends of Coker and DeVoe. The first thing they saw after climbing up the gangway of the *Cyclops* were the prisoners lined up on deck, wearing handcuffs and leg irons. Armed guards were posted around the vessel. Worley was wearing a forty-five.

Rumors flew about the ship: the passengers from the *Pittsburgh* would try to free their former shipmates; Lieutenant Forbes was still under arrest for telling of Worley, and the crew, once at sea, would seize the ship and free their executive officer; the prisoners had it better than the crew; Worley was going mad; Coker was to be transferred to the *Cyclops* for his execution. Every incident, no matter how minor, became fuel for the rumor mill the *Cyclops* had become.

After watching the *Pittsburgh* head out to sea, the *Cyclops'* passengers discovered that Commander Worley was wearing the forty-five automatic not because of the contingent of prisoners or his incarcerated executive officer. This was punishment day.

Those who were accused of infractions of the ship's (and Worley's) rules were to pay for their misdeeds. As their shipmates stood at ease, the accused were lined up at attention as Worley read the list of violations. All would be restricted to ship. However, those who had been before the captain previously were ordered to remove their shoes and stockings. Then, at pistol point, Worley drove the barefoot men around the ship's sunscorched steel decks. After a circuit around the ship, the men would return to their original standing place, where a seaman with a fire hose washed down their feet with cool seawater.

That same day the *Cyclops* weighed anchor and moved alongside a bulk cargo dock where she was to take on approximately eleven thousand tons of manganese ore. Manganese is a grayish white metallic substance that is added to other metals to give them a substantial increase in strength. Naval guns, large and small, are fabricated from manganese bronze. Ships' propellers and propeller shafts are also made of manganese bronze. The ore has a tremendous weight per cubic foot when compared to coal, which the *Cyclops* normally carried. Thus, the ship's holds were to be loaded by weight rather than volume. Manganese ore is also an abrasive with a tendency to settle down, creating a grinding action on whatever might be underneath. For these reasons, extra-heavy shorings and bracings must be used to prevent the cargo from shifting and reacting to the roll of a vessel at sea. Only one officer aboard the *Cyclops* was experienced in handling this type of cargo—Lieutenant Forbes. Before entering the naval service, he had spent a number of years on the Great Lakes as a master of vessels specializing in the transportation of heavy ores. But Forbes was still under arrest and confined to his quarters. To supervise the loading, Worley assigned a young lieutenant who had little, if any, experience in loading coal, let alone an exotic cargo such as manganese ore.

Inch by inch, the *Cyclops*'s hull pressed deeper into the water as ton after ton of the heavy bulk cargo poured into her seven holds. While the ship was being loaded, Ensign Nervig received orders transferring him to the USS *Glacier*, a supply ship. Receiving word of the transfer, Worley, who had been drinking heavily, became infuriated. Nervig's transfer meant that Worley was losing one of his few experienced officers and probably the only person in the crew he talked to on a personal basis. Worley contacted the admiral aboard the flagship of the South Atlantic Patrol Fleet in an attempt to keep Nervig aboard the *Cyclops*. But to Nervig's relief, the order was not rescinded.

Nervig probably knew the captain better than anyone else aboard the *Cyclops*. Nervig recalled a half century later: "He visited me every night when I had the dog watch. These visits lasted some two hours, and as we leaned against the forward bridge rail, he regaled me with stories of his home, family, and the many incidents of his long life at sea. He had a fund of tales, mostly humorous. I was fascinated by his experiences in the Philippines during the Spanish-American War when he commanded a troopship. These nocturnal visits became a regular routine, and I rather enjoyed them. His uniform, if it could be so called, never varied from the long underwear that he had worn on that first occasion. I have often wondered to what I owed these visits—his fondness for me or his sleeplessness." Although he was being transferred, Nervig would see the *Cyclops* once more before it met its eventual fate.

The collier's crew spent the next several days preparing the big ship for sea. As the water level neared her Plimsoll mark (a safety-load line painted on the sides of a ship's hull), hatches were not being battened down. But loading continued, and ultimately the Plimsoll mark was under water—signifying that the *Cyclops* was being overloaded. Why this blunder was permitted remains a mystery. Obviously, it was more than just an oversight, for even the least experienced seaman realizes that this is dangerous. Upon being loaded and readied for sea, the *Cyclops* cast off and headed up the coast for Brazil.

Since Brazil is south of the equator, February is midsummer there—the rainy season. On February 21, Lieutenant Nervig was standing at the bow of the *Glacier*, at anchor in the harbor at Bahia. Dressed in yellow foulweather gear, he was indistinguishable from the four enlisted men next to him. It had been drizzling steadily for several days. They had gone forward to make a routine check of the ship's anchor chain. Looking forward, Nervig saw the grayish black skeletal superstructure, which could only be the *Cyclops*, looming through the mist. Her twenty-four coaling booms were secured in seagoing position, the clamshell coal scoops were chained in place on deck, and all of the boats were lashed to their skids. The *Cyclops* was ready for her long voyage home.

What did Nervig think as he watched his former ship pushing against the outgoing tide? "As Bahia lies north of Rio de Janeiro, the *Cyclops* should have been approaching from the south," he told me. "But she stood in from the north. Again the familiar example of navigation as practiced aboard that vessel." The collier drifted to a halt, and the tranquil sound of the gentle pelting rain was shattered by the clanking of chain hurtling through the ship's hawsepipe. The *Cyclops* was at anchor.

Everyone who has ever served in the military has a memory of a friend or buddy who stands out in his mind above the recollection of anyone else regardless of how many years have gone by. Over a half century had passed since Conrad Nervig last saw his best friend, and yet he remembered it clearly. Ensign Carrol G. Page, the *Cyclop*'s paymaster, was the nephew of Senator Page, chairman of the Senate Naval Committee, and a scion of one of America's most politically prominent families. He had entered the navy as a commissioned officer, while Nervig was a "mustang" (navy and marine terminology for one who has worked his way up through the enlisted ranks to become a commissioned officer) who had joined the navy in 1907. In spite of their disparate backgrounds, they had spent hours discussing everything from Nervig's experiences in the "old navy" of the pre-war days to Page's Ivy League adventures.

The *Cyclops* received orders to sail for Baltimore on February 22. That morning, Ensign Page went aboard the *Glacier* to sign for some supplies issued to the *Cyclops*. "At his departure, I, as officer of the deck, escorted him to the gangway. On leaving, he grasped my hand in both of his and said very solemnly, 'Well, goodbye, old man, and God bless you.' I was deeply impressed with his finality, which was truly prophetic in its implication. I never saw Ensign Page again."

Still one more element was to be added to the already bizarre ship's complement before the *Cyclops*'s departure. Following a celebration at a private villa in Bahia, United States Consul General Alfred L. M. Gottschalk was driven to the navy pier in a 1916 Pierce Arrow limousine. Waiting for the car was a motorized whaleboat from the *Cyclops*. Standing in the stern sheets was Ensign Page, who had just been picked up at the *Glacier*. Also aboard were four of *Cyclops*'s crew who immediately started loading Gottschalk's trunks, bags, chests, and suitcases aboard the boat. After taking leave of friends who had accompanied him to the dock, the consul general boarded the boat and began his trip to the *Cyclops* and what was to be her enigmatic voyage into the history books.

Gottschalk boarded the gangway and climbed to the ship's main deck, where he was greeted by Worley wearing his dress whites. The ship had been scrubbed as clean as a coaling ship could get. The captain, apparently unconcerned about the rain, greeted his VIP passenger. Most of the crew, however, were quite aware of the weather, for they had been lined up in it for some time awaiting the consul general's arrival. The dignitary was shown his quarters and the crew allowed to break ranks. As the whaleboat was hoisted aboard, a bos'n's mate opened the steam valve at the anchor winch. In a matter of minutes the kerlunking noise of the machine was drowned out by the clanking of the anchor chain coming back up through the hawsepipe. Before the anchor was clear of the water, the ship began to vibrate to the throb of her propellers chopping through the water. The ship came about and headed seaward—taking 309 men on a voyage that would become one of the strangest unsolved mysteries of the sea.

Lieutenant Nervig stood on the *Glacier*'s bridge watching the *Cyclops* standing out to sea. As the ship disappeared into the mist and rain, he thought of the finality of his friend's farewell. With the last glimpse of the vessel before she was swallowed up in the rain, Nervig muttered aloud, "I bet there isn't a crewman aboard her who wouldn't give anything to change places with me right now."

By dawn the next day, the *Cyclops*, steaming north, was no longer in sight of land. Her orders were to proceed directly to Baltimore. She had taken aboard more than an adequate amount of coal and provisions for the voyage.

An early riser, Gottschalk was on deck at daybreak admiring the sunrise above the cloud-lined horizon, a spectacle that can be seen only in tropical and subtropical oceans. As the sun's intemperate heat began to overwhelm the lingering night-cooled air, the consul general sauntered down to the wardroom where he joined the ship's officers for breakfast. It was here that he became aware of the unusual circumstances concerning his forty-seven fellow passengers, the *Cyclops*, and her crew. He had known of the murder aboard the *Pittsburgh*, but it was only then that he learned that three of the four involved were aboard the same ship with him.

He was introduced to Lieutenant Forbes who, although still under arrest, was allowed to eat with the officers. As the day wore on, Gottschalk gradually became aware of the discontent among the ship's crew. A homeward-bound crew should be a happy crew, not filled with tense, dispirited men like these. And though it was traditional for a naval vessel to fly a "homeward-bound" pennant from her masthead, the *Cyclops* flew none.

As the *Cyclops* made her way north, she was still the subject of numerous rumors in the officers' clubs and waterfront bars of Brazil. One in particular was that the deserters would try to mutiny. Could this have been more than hearsay? Or was it typical navy scuttlebutt, in which five prisoners were amplified into a large number of mutineers? But if it was a rumor, what motivated it?

The *Cyclops* continued northward but at reduced speed, for the starboard engine, probably as a result of inadequate repairs in Rio de Janeiro, had broken down again. With only the port engine, her sustained speed was only eight knots. In addition, Captain Worley had been drinking to excess. He had been known throughout the fleet as the man who could match anyone glass for glass and get up and walk out seemingly unaffected. What caused him to guzzle more than his crew had ever seen him do before? Could it have been the trouble-plagued starboard engine? Could it have been the thought of his ship being overloaded? Then, too, there were the prisoners and, among the passengers, their friends from the *Pittsburgh*. The cruiser's commanding officer, Captain Bradshaw, had warned him not to take any chances. *Did some dissenting force rise among the prisoners, the passengers, the crew, or all three?* For although the ship had departed Brazil with more than enough coal and supplies to reach her destination, and Worley had orders to proceed directly to Baltimore without any stops, the *Cyclops* failed to do so.

Barbados is the easternmost island of the West Indies.

To the east lies nothing but open sea almost all the way to the Canary Islands off the coast of Africa. At the western end of Barbados is the island's largest city, Bridgetown, which overlooks Carlisle Bay. Early on Sunday morning, March 3, the *Cyclops* entered Carlisle Bay. The reverberations of the ship's anchor chain surging through her hawsepipe awakened the sleepy town. The inhabitants scurried to the waterfront—it was a rare occasion for a vessel that large to visit the island. The harbor could not accommodate a ship with the size and draft of the *Cyclops*, which had to anchor about a mile offshore. From her yardarm, she flew an English flag, a standard nautical courtesy to the British possession. As soon as the ship's identity became known to the island's officials, Brockholst Livingston, the United States consul at Barbados, boarded a launch along with customs officers and other island functionaries and headed out to the collier. After the usual handshaking and rituals of introduction, Livingston accompanied Worley to the captain's cabin under the ship's bridge. It was here that the consul was informed that the *Cyclops* had made her unscheduled call to pick up money, coal, and supplies to complete the voyage home.

Although Worley and the consul were mostly cordial, some words must have been exchanged when the former insisted on taking aboard large stores and foodstuffs, despite protests by Livingston about price and quantity.

After his meeting with Livingston and the completion of the routine customs check, Worley had some of the ship's boats launched and permitted members of the crew to have an eight-hour liberty. Apparently, the men who went ashore during the ship's two-day stopover caused little trouble, and all returned to the ship. But they did talk, for every bartender and anyone else who was anyone on the island knew of the executive officer's duress, the prisoners, the mechanical troubles, the crew's dislike of their captain, and hints of certain other odd happenings aboard the *Cyclops*.

The next afternoon, Livingston invited Worley, Gottschalk, and the ship's surgeon, Burt J. Asper, to the consulate for tea. The affair was cordial—there was no hint of any impending danger for the rest of the voyage, and the men from the ship seemed eager to get home. Before leaving, the three men signed the consul's daughter's autograph book. When the consul's young son, Brockholst Livingston III, returned from school, Worley told him all about the ship and life in the navy. A number of years later, young Livingston recalled: "About five o'clock our guests left, and we watched them from the beach as they went on board. There were some blasts on the whistles, and the *Cyclops* backed. Then, going ahead, she steamed *south*. We did not consider this course odd until a few weeks later. We got a cable from the State Department requesting full details of the ship's visit to Barbados." This was the last that was ever seen of the big ship, Worley, his crew, Gottschalk, the other passengers and the prisoners of the *Cyclops*.

All that is known is that the *Cyclops* had entered a section of the North Atlantic that would one day be referred to as "The Devil's Triangle."

The next day, March 5, the British liner *Vestris*, operated by the Lampert and Holt Lines, exchanged radio communications with the *Cyclops*. The latter reported "fair weather" and indicated no difficulties. The *Cyclops* was never heard from again. The United States Navy's largest collier was reported overdue on March 13, and immediately an intensive sea search was under way. Thousands and thousands of miles of the Atlantic Ocean were probed, but no trace of the ship was ever found.

In response to the cable to Livingston, the State Department received a most shocking reply:

SECRETARY OF STATE
Washington,
April 17, 2 P.M.

Department's 15th. Confidential. Master *Cyclops* stated that required 600 tons coal having sufficient to reach Bermuda. Engines very poor condition. Not sufficient funds and therefore requested payment by me—unusual. I have ascertained that he took here ton fresh meat, ton flour, thousand pounds vegetables, paying therefore 775 dollars. From different sources have learned the following. He had plenty of coal, alleged inferior; took coal, probably more than fifteen hundred tons. Master alluded to by others as damned Dutchman, apparently disliked by other officers. Rumored disturbances en route hither, men confined and one executed; also conspired [with] some prisoners from fleet in Brazilian waters, one [with] life sentence. United States Consul General Gottschalk passenger. 231 crew exclusive of officers and passengers. Have names [of] crew but not of all officers and passengers. Many Germanic names appear. Number telegraphic or wireless messages addressed master or in care of ship were delivered at this port. All telegrams for Barbados on file head office St. Thomas. I have to suggest scrutinizing these. While not having any definite grounds, I fear fate worse than sinking, though possibly based on instinctive dislike felt *towards master*.

LIVINGSTON, CONSUL

A clue to the *Cyclops*'s disappearance is contained in Livingston's cable to the State Department. Studying the cable segment by segment, these strange facts merit comment:

1. Captain Worley requested six hundred tons of coal, but fifteen hundred were loaded on the ship.

2. He stated that he needed six hundred tons to reach Bermuda. Why Bermuda? The safest and most practical route would be to skirt the Windward Islands, the Virgin Islands, Puerto Rico, Dominica, and eastern Cuba with the help of the following seas created by the easterly trade winds and then utilize the Gulf Stream's four-knot current northward through the Straits of Florida. Why risk voyaging out into the open Atlantic during wartime—especially with an overloaded ship? Especially during March when strong northeasterly winds are prevalent, and to venture out into the mid-Atlantic with only one engine functioning— unless . . .

3. The poor condition of the ship's engines and machinery could have completely disabled her at sea. But she had several complete sets of standby

batteries to operate the radio in such an emergency.

4. The additional provisions would not necessarily be of any significance, even though the ship had been fully provisioned upon departure from Brazil. A ton each of meat and flour would not go far among 308 men (assuming one was executed).

5. Had there been an execution aboard the *Cyclops*, it would have been the first navy shipboard hanging since 1849. However, would Worley have carried out an execution without a general court-martial and presidential approval? By law, both would have been required. Could many of the *Cyclops*'s crew members have gone ashore on liberty in Barbados with not one sailor's saying anything? Had it been done in secrecy, it would have been murder. Livingston reported only a rumor, but rare is the rumor that doesn't have at least a grain of truth to it.

6. Livingston also reported disturbances at sea. Consider the circumstances: a tyrannical captain, a skilled and well-liked officer unjustly under arrest, hardened prisoners having nothing to lose in an escape attempt, men aboard whose friends and former shipmates were imprisoned on the same ship, seamen seeing a shipmate illegally executed (if this ever did take place), and the general tension prevailing over the *Cyclops*. Almost anything could happen. Did anything happen? Or did Worley deliberately sail the *Cyclops* on a voyage of self-destruction? He did not know that he was scheduled to face a board of inquiry about his imperious treatment of his crew upon his return, he would have generally known the consequences to himself if an execution had taken place aboard his ship.

7. Although not mentioned in the consul's telegram, the ship was last seen steaming *south*, away from her destination. Was this the captain's deliberate decision or "again the familiar example of navigation as practiced aboard that vessel"? It might even have been a routine compass check, in the manner done aboard large ships to determine if any compass corrections are needed before starting a voyage.

8. Worley had been called a "damned Dutchman."

This was a World War I expression used by the Allies to denote the enemy. Although naval records showed that Worley was born in San Francisco, later investigation proved that he had been born in Germany and had illegally entered the United States in 1878, when he deserted a German merchant ship in San Francisco. Extensive investigation by the navy after the *Cyclops* disappeared revealed that Worley was actually named Johann Friedrich Georg Wichman. It was also brought out that whenever in port, even after he assumed command of the *Cyclops*, his closest male associates were German merchant captains. Could this, combined with the fact that before the United States entered the war, Consul General Gottschalk was fanatically pro-German and a number of the *Cyclops*'s crew were of German descent, have any connection with the ship's disappearance?

When the loss of the ship was made public, many people, both civilian and military, presumed that the vessel had been handed over to the enemy. So strong was this sentiment that within hours after the Armistice was signed ending World War I, Admiral William S. Sims, senior American naval officer in Europe, began an investigation of German naval files and records for any clue as to the fate of the *Cyclops*.

It was ascertained that the *Cyclops* never reached Germany and that there were no U-boats, surface raiders, or mines anywhere near the area where the big collier might have been steaming. However, a more determined investigation of the archives did reveal the name *Cyclops*. Far up in the North Atlantic, a U-boat commanded by a Lieutenant Doenitz, who would one day become Hitler's grand admiral, sank a British ship with all hands. Her name was *Cyclops*.

Theories, official and unofficial, materialized for years afterward. They varied from the German conspiracy to a sinking in a small but severe storm. Other theories blamed cargo shifting and turning the *Cyclops* turtle; or blamed the manganese ore grinding through the steel hull plates; or blamed the ship's small ammo locker exploding; or blamed mutineers sinking the ship with its crew and passengers and escaping in a small boat, and on and on. None could be documented.

As cited previously in analyzing Livingston's cable to the State Department, Worley was absolved by the government from any traitorous conspiracy with the Germans. However, in the September 1923 issue of *Naval Institute Proceedings*, there is an inconspicuous paragraph, a mention so vague and underplayed that it makes the reader wonder if there is more to it than meets the eye:

"A ship built at Brunswick, Georgia, and said to have carried a number of spies, is known to have been seized off Chesapeake about the time of the *Cyclops*'s disappearance. At least one important person with German connections is known to have been aboard the *Cyclops*."

There were only two important persons aboard the *Cyclops*—Gottschalk and Worley. Worley's German ties are known. What about the consul general? He was known to have been strongly pro-German before the war, and of German ancestry.

Ironically, there was still another development regarding the *Cyclops*. Two of her sister ships, the navy colliers *Nereus* and *Proteus*, were taken out of naval service during the early 1920s and laid up at the Norfolk Navy Yard until March 1941, when they were sold as surplus to Saguenay Terminals, Ltd., of Ottawa as bulk carriers. The entry of the United States into World War II overshadowed any mention in the press of the fate that befell these two ships. On November 23, 1941, the *Proteus* sailed from St. Thomas in the Virgin Islands with a cargo of bauxite bound for Norfolk. On December 10, the *Nereus* also departed St. Thomas bound for Norfolk with a cargo of bauxite. Both of the *Cyclops*'s sister ships also vanished without a trace.

German naval archives were investigated after World War II for clues as to the fate of the *Nereus* and the *Proteus*. The probe disclosed that at the time the two ships disappeared, there were no German U-boats, warships, or mines in that sector of the Atlantic and Caribbean. However, mention of the *Cyclops* did emerge. In January 1941, off Cape Sable, in the North Atlantic, a British ship was torpedoed with the loss of all ninety-four aboard. The ship's name was *Cyclops*.

Officially, how did the Navy feel about the loss of the *Cyclops*? To this very day, the United States Navy considers the disappearance of the USS *Cyclops* as the greatest unsolved mystery of the sea.

SIX

No Joy Aboard the *Joyita*

"The *Mary Celeste*!" That is the resounding response you'd get if you asked a hundred scholars of maritime phenomena to name the greatest unexplained ghost ship of the sea. Or at least ninety of the hundred would name that ship. The other ten, obviously more versed on the subject, would jump to their feet in protest. The room would echo with the name *Joyita*, a vessel whose identity has nearly evaporated into obscurity although it was once the feature story in a 1955 issue of *Life* magazine. "*Joyita*!" They would shout, and they would be right.

The *Mary Celeste* was found adrift six hundred miles west of Gibralter, with her holds flooded and not a soul aboard in 1872, long before the advent of airplanes and modern search and rescue techniques. But whatever happened aboard the *Joyita* occurred in an era of advanced radio communications, fairly accurate weather forecasts, and aircraft with efficient search and rescue equipment.

It has been almost definitely concluded that those

aboard the *Mary Celeste* put off in one of the vessel's
lifeboats to escape fumes emanating from leaking casks
of alcohol stored in one of the holds. Before the fumes
dissipated and the crew could return to the ship, however, the lifeboat and ship became seperated due to a
sudden incidence of bad weather. Nevertheless, today
the *Mary Celeste* remains a classic mystery tale of the
sea.

The *Joyita* (Spanish for "little jewel") was found in a
derelict condition at dawn on November 10, 1955, in the
South Pacific, ninety miles north of Fiji. The 69-foot
vessel was discovered, with a 55-degree port list and one
rail awash by Captain Gerald Douglas of the interisland
freighter *Tuvalu* (wrecked twelve years later off the
coast of New Zealand).

The Fiji government at Suva received the following
message from Captain Douglas: "*Joyita* found half waterlogged in position 14 degrees, 42 minutes south and
179 degrees and 45 minutes east by dead reckoning.
Boat sent across, but nobody aboard. Bodies possibly in
flooded compartment. Portside superstructure, including
funnel, blown away. Canvas awning rigged apparently
subsequent to accident. No logbook or message found.
Joyita constitutes hazard to shipping. Consider feasible
tow to sheltered anchorage. Fiji waters thirty hours. Will
standby until advised."

On Monday, October 3, 1955, the *Joyita* had put to sea
from Apia Harbor, Western Samoa, for *Fakaofo*, where
she would pick up seventy tons of copra (dried coconut
meat). In addition to a crew of six, she carried nine la-
borors and nine passengers, including District Governor
R. D. Pearless, who had just arrived from New Zealand.
Most of the others were Gilbert or Tokelau islanders. Of

the twenty-five people aboard the *Joyita*, probably only her skipper, Thomas Henry "Dusty" Miller, 39, a World War II Royal Navy veteran, was aware that the vessel had been cursed ever since she was first launched.

Originally built as a palatial yacht for Hollywood film director and producer Roland West, the *Joyita* was launched at Wilmington Boat Works of Los Angeles in 1931. West chose the name *Joyita* for an actress friend with whom he had been intimate. The yacht was registered in Jewel Carmen's name in 1932. Just before the launching, a shipfitter of Portuguese descent fell from the vessel's superstructure onto the marine railway tracks below. He died instantly from a severed spine and broken neck.

Shortly after the accident, the worker's widow came down to the yard and proclaimed that her husband had died because work on the yacht was being rushed by the builders. She was screaming and making a scene. Upon being asked to leave the boatyard, she placed an ancient Portuguese curse on the *Joyita*.

Within a year, the romance between West and Jewel Carmen began to wither, and the RKO producer repossessed the *Joyita*. On her first offshore voyage, a short cruise to Catalina Island in 1932, a ruinous fire broke out in the engine room, and the yacht had to be towed back to port. After the fire damage was repaired, the vessel was sold and used for charter service. Among the notable Hollywood celebrities who used the *Joyita* were Mary Pickford, Douglas Fairbanks, and Ronald Colman. Both Humphery Bogart and Errol Flynn had considered buying the boat. However, they changed their minds after a guest mysteriously disappeared from the vessel off Catalina Island.

During World War II, the *Joyita* was taken over by the United States Navy and used for a patrol boat (YP) at Pearl Harbor. During this period, she ran aground several times and had to be drydocked. After the war, she was sold as surplus when her civilian owner said that he didn't want her back.

In 1947, a caretaker was overcome by battery acid fumes in the engine room and died an agonizing death aboard the *Joyita*. On another occassion, her mooring lines parted, and she drifted into another vessel. Then two drunks had a bloody knife fight aboard her. Each man critically wounded the other.

After discovering her wallowing at sea, Captain Douglas towed the *Joyita* to Suva, where she was pumped dry. On November 14, marine surveyors began their inspection of the vessel. In one hold, they found a number of empty fuel oil drums; in another, bales of burlap copra bags. No bodies were found anywhere aboard the little ship. The rudder had been damaged and was jammed hard to the port. A set of signal flags was found tangled in a mass of rigging. The flags had been hung in order, spelling out WNQV. No one could figure out the meaning of the message. Smashed in the scuppers was the *Joyita*'s ship-to-shore radio. The hands of both ship's clocks were stopped at two minutes before ten. All switches and controls remained in the "on" position. The electric stove in the galley was set at "high." Where was the logbook? The inspectors were unable to locate it.

The assistant harbormaster at Suva, Captain E. L. James, found the probable reason why the *Joyita* had taken on so much water—a broken seawater pipe in the engine room. Examination revealed that the leak developed from two dissimilar metal fittings being fastened together. This had generated an electrolytical reaction which had corroded the fittings. There were some who questioned how the corroded water connection had kept ahead of the bilge pumps and caused the *Joyita* to take on so much water. Of more concern, however, was what happened to the twenty-five persons aboard her.

The *Joyita* was believed to be unsinkable, a belief legitimized by the fact that she remained afloat while full of water. The thick cork insultaion around her holds, the empty oil drums inside the holds, and the heavy timbers used in her construction all contributed to the *Joyita*'s remaining afloat. Captain Miller was completely aware of his ship's buoyancy. And certainly the vessel's bilge pumps could have overridden any leaking or broken pipe. So why did the twenty-five people aboard flee the unsinkable ship in what must have been three very overcrowded life rafts?

The *Joyita* carried a deck cargo of 2,000 board feet of lumber along with the numerous empty oil drums. These items, all buoyant, were never found, nor were the life rafts or life preservers. Missing from the cargo hold were seven cases of aluminum stripping to be used as rat guards around coconut trees and seventy sacks of rice, sugar, and flour. Each bag weighed fifty to one hundred pounds. It is unlikely that these items of cargo could have been carried away in three overcrowded life rafts. One of the passengers, G. K. Williams, a copra buyer, had been carrying £50 in silver and £950 in banknotes. None of his money was found aboard.

After checking over the hulk of the *Joyita*, the examiners began to assemble the facts concerning the vessel's mysterious voyage. When the *Joyita* put out from

Apia, only one of her two engines was operational. The other had a defective clutch mechanism that Dusty Miller had planned to repair while the vessel was under way. The *Joyita* had been lying idle in the harbor for at least five months before her final voyage, since creditors had placed a lien on the vessel that restricted her from leaving port. Thus, the *Joyita* had fallen into semidisrepair. The authorities even attempted to prevent her from sailing, but the creditors finally agreed that profits from the trip would earn at least some of their money back.

As the *Joyita* was preparing to cast off, an old Samoan woman ran down to the dock screeching hysterically for her nephew, who was a passenger aboard the vessel. She screamed that the *Joyita* was under an evil spell. In vain, she pleaded with her nephew to leave the ship; however, he chose to remain aboard when they pulled away from the dock.

An Australian seaman who had made a number of voyages aboard the *Joyita* came forward and told of the voyages he had made with Dusty (the nickname given Captain Miller by his friends) in the past. William B. Menard of Hawaii did a considerable amount of research on the *Joyita*. In one of his many articles, he quotes the Australian.

"Twice, quite a way out of Pago, we were followed by a ship without lights. When I told Dusty we were being followed, he looked the other ship over with his binoculars. His face went white, and his knees caved under him. I don't know if he recognized the vessel or not, but he did get excited. He ordered the running lights turned off, and he took over the helm himself, heading the *Joyita* into a nearby rain squall. So, anyways, we were able to get away from whoever was following us.

"The next time I discovered that we were being shadowed was just before dark. I saw this vessel silhouetted on the horizon. I studied her through my binoculars. I couldn't believe what I saw. It looked like an old Spanish galleon—like Columbus used. I figured it had to be one of those Japanese tuna boats with a high superstructure aft. It kept shadowing us. We made it into Apia Harbor before the mystery vessel could catch us. Dusty was real shaken over that second shadowing.

"Several months later, he asked me if I knew what a Portuguese galleon looked like and if I thought the ship trailing us looked like one. He never brought the subject up again."

Could the ghost of a Portuguese galleon have had anything to do with the curse placed on the *Joyita* twenty-four years earlier by an hysterical, grieving Portuguese widow?

On December 28, 1955, during the investigation of the *Joyita*, another interisland freighter, the M/S *Arakarimoa*, sailed from Tarawa for Maiana in the Gilbert Islands with fifteen crew and eight passengers. Her cargo consisted mainly of copra sacks. Sailing with the *Arakarimoa* was her sister ship, the *Aratoba*. The two vessels were in sight of each other during the first day until shortly before midnight, when the *Arakarimoa* pulled ahead and on into the darkness.

When the *Aratoba* arrived at their destination, the *Arakarimoa* had not arrived, nor had any word been heard from her. Search craft could find no trace of the overdue ship.

Several months later, a battered hull was found awash on a coral reef. Although there was not enough left of the hulk for identification, the general feeling was that it was the *Arakarimoa*. However, if it was that ship, there was no indication whatsoever as to the fate of the twenty-three persons who had been aboard her.

Meanwhile, numerous theories concerning the fate of those aboard the *Joyita* arose back in Apia. One was that everyone had been washed overboard by a giant freak wave or a waterspout. Another was that a giant undersea volcano had erupted directly under the *Joyita*. (This had happened to a Tongan vessel six months previously.) In that incident, all but two of those who had been swept over the side were able to make it back aboard.) Russian submarines were featured in another theory, for several had been sighted in the area around that time. Smugglers and sea monsters were also mentioned. And, of course, UFO buffs had a field day. Another speculation was that pirates had strayed out of their Malayan home waters. Mutiny and murder on the high seas were not excluded. None of these theories, however, was ever conclusively accepted.

Captain Dusty Miller was just what a Hollywood casting director would envision as the captain of a south seas interisland freighter. He was solidly built and of medium height. His sun-tanned skin blended well with that of the Samoans. The dark brown hair on his head was starting to thin. His eyes were in a perpetual squint as a result of many years' exposure to the tropical sun. His handlebar mustache was typically old British. But more than anything else, it was the lavalava (sarong) hanging from his hips that indicated that the thirty-nine-year-old British man had gone native.

William B. Menard, in another of his articles, tells of a conversation that he had with Miller. The captain told

Menard of the financial troubles and bad luck he was having with the *Joyita*. The vessel's creditors were making it difficult to find a charter. Dusty Miller said, "I'm not sure, but there is something satanic about the *Joyita*. At night when I lay in my bunk aboard her, I have a feeling or sense of not being alone. The whole vessel seems permeated with it. I've never sensed something so devilish before. Sometimes I hear voices . . . maybe a woman laughing. There's some kind of unearthly atmosphere aboard her. It hasn't been a good luck vessel for me."

Was the *Joyita* just another victim of the unrelenting sea? Or did the curse of the Portuguese widow doom her?

After the mystery of the *Joyita* simmered down, a group of planters purchased the vessel and completely rebuilt her. But there was still to be no peace for the *Joyita*. In 1957, while plying through the Koro Sea, she piled up on the dangerous Horseshoe Reef. She was salvaged and again placed back in service.

In 1959, the *Joyita* once again ran onto a reef near Makongai in the Fiji Islands. Her owners abandoned her after having her towed onto a beach.

After many months of exposure to weather and sea, the *Joyita* was again given a new life. This time she was purchased by Viscount Robert Cecil Romer Maugham, barrister-at-law, author, and nephew of Somerset Maugham. His plan was to write a movie script about the enigmatic life of the *Joyita*. Although the project never progressed beyond the script stage, Maugham did manage to publish two books about the vessel, *The Joyita Mystery*, which was nonfiction, and *November Reef*, a novel. During this time, the *Joyita* still lay aground as the elements took their toll. But, once again, the *Joyita* would be reprieved.

In September 1966, a Major Casling-Cottle, who operated a tourist attraction on Levuka with his wife and daughter, purchased the hulk for little more than scrap price. He intended to use her as an exhibit in their museum of strange mysteries of the sea.

There is little doubt about the *Joyita*'s being one of the most notorious of all jinxed ships. Her infamy even surpasses that of the strangely afflicted *Great Eastern* in the late 1800s. In the annals of the sea there have been many bad-luck ships, and the *Joyita* ranks with the most enigmatic, those that left too many confusing questions, never to be answered.

SEVEN

The Mail Came Through—
But the Crew Didn't

The Bahama Islands are considered to have the finest, safest waters in all the oceans. Thousands and thousands of yachts and other small craft cruise the area each year. One is seldom more than a day from land and in most cases only a few hours away. Except during inclement weather, the waters are crystal clear. Many movies supposedly filmed underwater in other parts of the world are actually filmed here. Not only are the islands a mecca for yachtsmen, but well over a million and a half tourists, arriving by cruise ships and airplanes, visit the islands annually. The Bahamas consist of six hundred islands and 2,387 uninhabited rocky cays. Starting from Bimini, forty-five miles east of Miami, they extend for six hundred miles to the east and the same distance north and south from Walker Cay to Great Inagua. They are peaceful. They are near tropical. And they are tranquilizing. But unromantic things do happen in the Bahamas.

Boats get wrecked on reefs. Others get lost and have

to be rescued by the United States Coast Guard or the Bahama Air Sea Rescue Service. Airplanes attempting to fly through squalls are forced down at sea. On occasion, hurricanes strike the area, wiping out whole harbors—boats, docks, and all. And from time to time an airplane, yacht, or ship simply disappears without a trace. All over these lush, semitropical islands there are shells of little pink or white houses whose owners never came home from the sea—for all of the Bahamas are in the Devil's Triangle.

The economic and political center of the islands is Nassau, which lies south and approximately 150 miles east of Miami. Five hundred miles to the southeast of Nassau are the Turks Islands. Although not politically part of the Bahamas, they are geographically the easternmost group. Politically, the people are Jamaican, and these islands are an affiliate of the Jamaican government. The two Turks Islands, Grand Turk and Little Turk, are bleak and barren. Until the 1960s their eight hundred residents derived meager incomes harvesting salt from the numerous salt ponds abounding on the islands, fishing, and raising cattle, sheep, and pigs. Until tourism began to spread into the Turks and the neighboring Caicos Islands in the 1970s, the biggest event in the lives of the islanders was saving enough money to make a pilgrimage to Nassau about once every five years. There is no harbor as such in the Turks. Larger vessels calling there anchor off the settlement of Cockburn Town. Transportation between ships and the island is by small boat.

On December 2, 1946, the two-masted schooner *City Belle*, en route from the Dominican Republic to Nassau, paid a call at Cockburn Town with a cargo of lumber.

The anchor had no sooner been dropped than the ship was surrounded by a fleet of small boats that had come to unload several thousand board feet of lumber. The work progressed with great haste, for the halo around the afternoon sun meant but one thing to the native crews—the weather was changing for the worse. The waters surrounding the Turks Islands were not the best place for a 120-foot-long deep draft schooner to be caught during dirty weather. After expeditiously off-loading the last of consignment destined for the island, the final boat, loaded to the gunwales, headed for shore. By now the prevailing southeast wind had veered to the south. By nightfall or early morning, it would work around to the west, and then to the north, bringing in a cold front.

Four members of the schooner's ten-man crew were already leaning on their capstan bars, ready to hoist anchor. Several hands were busily passing mail sacks bound for Nassau into the forward hold where the lumber had been.

Beating its way out to the *City Belle* from the only dock at Cockburn Town was a native fishing smack no longer than twenty-two feet from stem to stern and with a beam one-third that size. Her sails were a seagoing quilt, as patches had replaced nearly all of the original canvas. In addition to the two-man crew there were twenty-two vacation-bound passengers—men, women and children—aboard the small craft. They were sitting along both gunwales, on the bowsprit, in the bottom, and atop each other. An occasional wave would pour over the gunwales. When too much water had accumulated in the bilge, several passengers would swing their legs over the side, to let others bail out the water with old rusty paint cans. Then the dangling legs would swing back aboard. This occurred at least every five minutes during the boat's thirty-minute trip out to the schooner. The passengers' luggage, consisting of a few vintage suitcases—the kind salesmen use for samples—several dozen straw bags jam-packed full of clothes, food, live chickens and other items lay in the sloshing bilge water. They were looking forward to spending Christmas in Nassau.

As the little boat with its human cargo banged against the nineteen-inch tires swinging from the schooner's side, her patchwork sail was dropped. The twenty-two eager passengers scampered and helped each other over the ship's bulwark. Crying babies and wet cackling chickens were passed from arm to arm. Suitcases and straw bags, getting lighter by the second as the water drained from them, were taken aboard last.

As the "commuter" boat cast off for shore, the capstan crew began hoisting the anchor. As the fore and head-sails were hoisted, the mainsail, which had been holding the vessel's bow into the wind, was slackened off, and the big schooner was under way.

The next morning the *City Belle* was close hauled and beating into a northerly wind as she worked her way across the Crooked Island Passage toward the Exuma Islands. That's when it happened.

On December 5, 1946, seventy-four years to the day after the deserted, derelict *Mary Celeste* was discovered with all hands missing, and exactly one year after an ill-fated flight of five U.S. Navy planes took off from Fort Lauderdale, never to be seen again, the schooner *City Belle* was found adrift and completely deserted about three hundred miles southeast of Miami. A crash boat from the U.S. Naval Base on Great Exuma Island had discovered the forsaken sailing ship while on a routine patrol. It had been three days since the schooner had departed the Turks Islands. There had not been any violence aboard. Her cargo was intact. And the ship was in a seaworthy condition. The records and mail were removed and delivered to the British commissioner at Great Exuma. The ship's log gave no clue as to why the *City Belle* was abandoned. Everything aboard, including the passengers' baggage, was shipshape. The only life aboard were the cackling chickens parading along her main deck. Only the lifeboats were missing.

An immediate sea and air search commenced. Every island, even some that were quite far from the schooner's track, was searched. Natives passed word from island to island, but no trace of either survivors or lifeboats was ever found. Speculation in Nassau shipping circles centered on the possibility that the thirty-two crewmen and passengers had panicked and abandoned ship during the high winds accompanying the cold front that had whipped up those waters for three days. Yet the *City Belle*, when found, was not in any danger of foundering. Had she been discovered by a private vessel, rather than a government, lore and salvage claims had led to an admiralty court hearing, there is little doubt that the mystery of the *City Belle* would rival that of the *Mary Celeste* in notoriety.

Another maritime mystery centers around a different schooner—the five-master *Carroll A. Deering*. She hailed from Portland, Maine, and was owned by the C. G. Deering Co. Commanding her was Captain Willis B. Wormwell. Charging through the waves under full sail, she was, even for her day, one of the most picturesque vessels afloat.

However, so baffling was the mystery surrounding this ship that five different United States government departments investigated the case. They included the State Department, the Treasury, the Navy, the Department of Commerce, and the Justice Department. Their combined consensus was that the *Carroll A. Deering* had been a victim of a terrifying experience, the likes of which hadn't been reported in over 100 years.

The schooner had departed Norfolk, Virginia, in September 1920, bound for Rio de Janeiro with a cargo of general merchandise and coal. Upon arrival in Brazil, the *Deering* was immediately off-loaded. She then took aboard another cargo destined for Norfolk. The schooner departed from Rio de Janeiro on December 2, for Barbados.

When the *Deering* lay at anchor off Bridgetown during the first week of January 1921, rumors circulated about Captain Wormwell's having had problems with some members of the crew en route to the island. That was a familiar story, for three years earlier another ship had arrived at this same island from Rio de Janeiro with similar rumors of disturbances en route. The other vessel's voyage had originated in Norfolk with a cargo of coal. She had sailed to Rio, departed that port for Barbados, and then set off for Norfolk. She was, of course, the *Cyclops*.

Before the *Deering* sailed from Barbados, Captain Wormwell had to bail his hard-drinking second mate, Charles McLellan, out of jail for drunk and disorderly conduct. With half the crew drunk, the schooner departed for Norfolk on January 9, still following the track of the *Cyclops*.

On the afternoon of January 23, 1921, the *Deering* sailed past the lightship *Cape Fear* off the North Carolina coast. The men aboard the lightship noticed nothing unusual as the big schooner passed. Four days later, hurricane-force winds ripped down the North Carolina coastline. By January 29, the winds had diminished somewhat, but sea conditions were still far from ideal. On that afternoon, the *Deering* approached the lightship *Cape Lookout* off Diamond Shoals, about ninety miles from Cape Fear. She was moving at a speed of five knots as she closed the distance to the lightship. When the two vessels were within hailing, a man with red hair aboard the schooner, who was definitely not Captain Wormwell, yelled across to the captain of the lightship, Thomas Jacobson, "We lost both anchors while riding out the storm. Can you report it ashore for us?" The others aboard the schooner said nothing.

Captain Jacobson later testified that the man did not give the impression of being a ship's officer and spoke with a foreign accent. The lightship's captain was unable to send the message, since his wireless was not working. Aside from her missing anchors, the *Deering* appeared to be in good condition.

A short time after the schooner sailed past the lightship, an unidentified steamship passed. The lightship signalled her to take a message, but the signal was ignored. Numerous attempts were made by the lightship to communicate with the steamer, but no response was received. She continued to steam on, following the same track as the *Deering*. In desperation, Captain Jacobson blasted away four times on his whistle, an international emergency signal. Still he was ignored.

As day broke on January 31, the men who manned the Diamond Shoals lifesaving station discovered a five-masted schooner hard up on the shoals along the outer banks. All sails were set except the two forward jibs. Big waves were sweeping the length of the schooner's decks. The men from the lifesaving station attempted to reach the grounded vessel in their surfboat, but high seas prevented them from boarding her. They could see, however, that the vessel was abandoned and that the lifeboats were gone. For four days, the breaking seas lashed the schooner, as howling winds ripped her beating sails into shreds.

When the seas finally abated to a point where the *Deering* could be boarded, members of the lifesaving station crew and Coast Guard officials inspected her. Aside from two cats that had somehow managed to survive the punishing seas that had been sweeping over the vessel, she was completely abandoned. Apparently, the crew had abandoned ship in a hurry. There was evidence that a meal was being prepared at the time the mysterious incident occurred. Most of the provisions, clothing, and supplies had been removed. The *Deering*'s rudder and steering mechanism had been damaged during the grounding. The binnacle and compass had been smashed, drawers and cabinets were left open, and a general disorderliness prevailed throughout the schooner. The motor lifeboat and dory were missing, as were most of the charts, the log, and the navigation instruments. The crew was never seen again, and the two boats (or their wreckage) were never found.

A number of months passed before the press jumped

on the story. A front page *New York Times* story date-lined Washington, June 20, 1921, stated, "The crew of an American ship is missing, and what seems to be con-clusive evidence has been obtained that the men were taken as prisoners to another vessel and carried away to parts unknown, if they were not murdered."

Captain O. W. Parker of the Marine Shipping Board stated, "Piracy without a doubt still exists as it has since the days of the Phoenicians." Shipowners were divided in their opinions. Some thought it unlikely that pirates and sea robbers could prey on ships in the twentieth century when wireless apparatus aboard vessels was be-coming almost universal, commerce lanes on the high seas were more crowded than ever, and international pa-trols kept close watch on what was going on. Other ship-pers attributed unexplained shipping losses to World War I mines that eventually separated from their moor-ings and floated about the sea. But ship owners familiar with tramp steamers and sailing vessels continued to be-lieve that piracy had again reared its ugly head.

On June 22, the *Times* carried the following headline: "More Ships Added to Mystery List." Between October 1920 and February 1921 at least ten ships vanished in the western Atlantic. But they received little attention in the press until the *Carroll A. Deering* became a front-page story.

The item that most fueled the theory of piracy and kidnapping on the high seas was a bottle with a note in it that was found on the beach at Buxton, North Caro-lina, on April 11, by Christopher Columbus Gray. The message read, "Deering captured by oil-burning boat-like chaser, taking off everything, handcuffing crew. Crew hiding all over ship. No chance to make escape.

Finder please notify headquarters of Deering." Many scoffed at the message as a hoax. But was it?

Facing skepticism and ridicule, Mrs. W. B. Wormwell, wife of the schooner's captain, followed up one clue after another with the skill of Sherlock Holmes. She approached the family of each of the missing crew members and obtained a handwriting sample of every man who crewed on the *Deering*. The vessel's owners provided her with signatures obtained when the men signed aboard the ship. The customs house in Norfolk gave her the note that was found in the bottle. Armed with the message and the handwriting samples, she had three different handwriting experts analyze the writings. They confirmed her previous suspicion that the note was written by Henry Bates of Islesboro, Maine, the schooner's engineer (as engineer on a sailing vessel, he would have maintained the lifeboat motor and the deck machinery). Mrs. Wormwell also learned from experts in Washington, who had examined both the paper and the bottle, that the paper was made in Norway and imported to Brazil in large quantities. She was also informed that the bottle was manufactured in Brazil. These facts, combined with the lightship's report of the strange steamer following the *Deering*, pointed to piracy.

Although it was proven that the bottle and its message were authentic, nothing has ever been published by either the press or the government about the fate of the missing crew. It is possible that the men serving aboard the *Carroll A. Deering* were kidnapped and more than likely slain by their abductors. During Prohibition, Barbados, like most other West Indian islands, was a stepping-off place for U.S.-bound rumrunners. A vessel the size of the *Deering* could easily transport enough liquor to be worth well over a million dollars once ashore in the United States.

Just outside the twelve-mile limit of the eastern seaboard was an area known as "Rum Row" where the contraband cargos were transferred to smaller vessels for the dash in to shore. Many foreigners were engaged in the trade, including a number of "big-fisted, rough-and-tumble" Finns. Because the hoodlum element would go through anything, including murder, to get their illegal cargos ashore, they were referred to as the "go through guys." There are cases on record where "go through guys" murdered crews of larger ships bringing the liquor to "Rum Row" if they thought the cargo was worth the risk. Sometimes inexperienced rumrunners were hijacked, and if the crews resisted, they were murdered. It is not beyond the realm of possibility that the crew of the *Carroll A. Deering*, enticed by the thought of big profits, took on a load of illegal liquor at Barbados or even in South America and had a confrontation with the "go through guys" as their ship approached "Rum Row." Some people in the trade had obtained World War I surplus subchasers such as the "boat-like chaser" mentioned in the bottle message.

A later check revealed that there was no one among the crew of the *Deering* who spoke with a foreign accent or had red hair like the man who spoke to the lightship. Could the men seen on the schooner's deck by the lightship crew have been hijackers waiting to be taken off by their own ship—the strange steamer that appeared shortly afterward?

EIGHT

Skeletons at Sea

"There was nothing left of them but a bag of bones. It appears that they had been out there at sea for ages." That is how Henry Conrad, a special agent for the United States Customs Service, described what he first saw when boarding the yacht *Grace A. Ghislaine*.

A gentle easterly breeze was blowing across the Gulf of Mexico as the shrimp boat *Warrior III* plied into oncoming waves as she motored back to her home port of Tampa, 800 miles to the east. It was the morning of Wednesday, June 18, 1975, and the crew was hoping to make it back to Florida in time for the weekend. Humidity from scattered rain squalls made the crew lackadaisical—a mood that was not to last for long.

The white and blue vessel was about sixty miles northeast of the Yucatan Peninsula. Ahead were the remnants of a series of rapidly diminishing rain squalls. Off to port, there appeared to be a small boat that was partially obscured by a rain shower. With one hand still on the wheel, the shrimper's skipper, Addis Sylvester

McGinn III of Little River, South Carolina, reached for his binoculars. Looking through his glasses, McGinn saw what looked like a small sailboat—a derelict sailboat. As the *Warrior III* drew closer to the craft, the crew, lining the rail, could read the name painted on its bow, *Grace A. Ghislaine*, and the registration numbers "FDF-8786." McGinn recognized the letters as being of French origin.

Fort de France, located on the French island of Martinique, is the chief city of the Antilles, located in the southeastern sector of the Caribbean, some two thousand miles from the Yucatan Peninsula. It is a long voyage from the sun-bleached islands of the Antilles to the hot and humid coast of southeast Mexico. The twenty-foot sloop *Grace A. Ghislaine*, out of Fort de France, made that journey. There is nothing unusual about a twenty-two foot boat making a two-thousand mile ocean voyage—boats half that size have crossed the Atlantic— unless it is made under mysterious circumstances. And the cruise of the *Grace A. Ghislaine* was a voyage of mystery.

Captain McGinn maneuvered the *Warrior III* closer to the pitching sloop. Tattered rags that were once sails fluttered in the breeze like the wings of an injured bird trying to take flight. The rudder and its tiller handle wobbled sloppily from side to side. No one could be seen aboard the seemingly abandoned boat. Sloshing water gurgled through her half filled bilges.

As the shrimp boat eased alongside the wallowing sailboat, a crewman from the shrimper jumped aboard the sloop. He began bailing out some of the water so the sloop could be lifted aboard the *Warrior III*. As the water began to recede, the fisherman saw something just below its surface. He bailed faster. Soon he knew what he was looking at. The little boat did have a crew. She had been manned by a crew of the dead—*skeletons*. Two skeletons, their bones picked clean, probably by sea birds, and bleached white by the relentless tropical sun, lay in the bottom of the *Grace A. Ghislaine*. Only a few rotted rags remained of their clothing. Among the items found aboard the boat were a commercial-type fishing net, a few French coins, and two calendar wristwatches. One was stopped on the twelfth and the other on the thirteenth. But there was no indication as to the month. The boat with its dead crew was hoisted aboard the shrimper and taken to Tampa.

Customs and FBI officials examined the craft upon its arrival in Florida. A coast guard report from San Juan stated that the boat could be one that sailed from Martinique and had been missing since April 12, two months earlier. Whatever happened to the *Grace A. Ghislaine* must have occurred some time before the vessel was swept into the Gulf of Mexico by the southeast trade winds. There was no visible evidence of foul play, and there was still some food and drinking water aboard. It appeared that they had just gone out for a day sail—a two-thousand-mile day sail.

NINE

Floating Caskets

The *Sky Plover*'s bow barely made a wake as it sliced
through the calm waters of the Gulf Stream. The
schooner, heaving on the easy swells rolling in from the
east, had been ghosting along at less than two knots for
several days. With the exception of the usual summer-
time thunderheads far astern toward the Bahamas, the
sky was cloudless. Ahead, just on the horizon, lay a dark
green streak that was the Miami shoreline. Its regularity
was broken only by the Cape Florida lighthouse pointing
skyward and the break that was Biscayne Channel. The
gentle southeasterly breeze was giving the schooner only
enough way to maintain steerage. It was a lazy day. For
those not in a hurry, it could have been called a perfect
day, but that afternoon in 1906 was not perfect for the
men looking down at the water from the deck of the *Sky
Plover.*

The crew had just finished their noon meal when the
lookout bellowed from the masthead, "Wreckage two
points off the port bow!"

The captain looked up at the man aloft and then in the direction to which he was pointing. The helmsman was ordered to put the wheel over and head the ship on that bearing.

Ten minutes later the crew, who only a little while earlier had anticipated a possible salvage recovery, looked forlornly down into the water. Some of their faces expressed awe—others, terror.

"Treasure chests!" shouted the cabin boy.

"Coffins!" a chorus of other voices gasped in unison.

And coffins they were. The crew of the *Sky Plover* counted at least four barnacle-encrusted caskets tossing gently about in the nearly smooth sea. No attempt was made to recover any of the floating coffins.

Word that the *Sky Plover* had discovered drifting caskets reached Miami well ahead of the vessel, for the crew of Captain Bravo's pilot boat learned of the incident when the harbor pilot boarded the schooner, and in the light air the pilot boat reached the dock half an hour before the schooner. After the *Sky Plover*'s cargo, a disassembled sawmill, was unloaded, the stevedores began loading her outgoing cargo of sisal and fresh pineapples. The longshoremen, most of whom were "sailors on the beach," predicted that sighting the caskets was a bad omen for the schooner. Speculation about the origin of the coffins was heard along the Miami waterfront for months afterward.

In 1841, a son, Charles Francis, was born to the John Coghlans, Irish immigrants living on Prince Edward Island, off Canada's eastern coast. Charles Francis possessed a remarkable dramatic talent. In fact, his playacting ability was so exceptional that when he was fourteen, friends and relatives gathered together enough money to send him to England to study for a theatrical career. When the day came for Charles Francis to sail off, he stood at the end of the pier, looked around at the pine-covered countryside, then turned to his benefactors and said, "If I achieve fame and glory in the theatre, I shall one day return to this place of my birth, no matter what odds I might encounter. God will bring me home."

By the time Charles Francis Coghlan reached his nineteenth birthday, he was appearing on the stage in London. Before he was twenty-five, he had become a renowned Shakespearean actor. At thirty, he was considered the greatest Shakespearean actor in the English theater.

His fame spread across the Atlantic, and he was invited to perform in New York City. He loved America, and America loved him. Coghlan played lead roles opposite such theatrical greats as Miss Lily Langtry and Mrs. Harrison Fiske. Eventually, he organized his own troupe, one that specialized in Shakespearean drama. From Broadway to the roughest cow towns he received standing ovations.

Like most actors and actresses of the nineteenth century, however, Charles Francis Coghlan was superstitious. He regularly consulted astrologers, fortune-tellers, and seers. One whom he visited periodically gave him a rather bizarre prediction: "You will never live to see the twentieth century. You will be interred in a city in the South, but a great storm will beset that city, and your remains will be cast upon the sea." With a show-must-go-on spirit, however, Coghlan did not let the prophecy bother him, and he continued appearing on the stage throughout the United States.

On November 27, 1899, Charles Coghlan's theatrical company was presenting a performance of *Hamlet* in Galveston, Texas. That evening, shortly before curtain call, Coghlan complained of feeling ill. After being assured that his understudy could carry on, he was taken to his hotel room. Whether Charles Francis Coghlan gave any thought that evening to the prediction made by his spiritual consultant a decade earlier is not known, but shortly after midnight he died. He was buried in a copper-lined cypress coffin.

On August 27, 1900, far out in the Atlantic Ocean, halfway between Africa and the West Indies, a tropical storm was born. By the time it reached the Caribbean, it had become a full-grown hurricane. As the storm moved into the Gulf of Mexico, the wind gusts were nearing two hundred miles per hour. The barometer at Galveston fell to 27.64 inches. When the great hurricane struck on September 8, it was accompanied by a storm tide that exceeded twenty feet in height. Damage amounted to more than thirty million dollars. Nearly five thousand buildings were demolished by wind and water. Over six thousand lives, almost one-sixth of the city's population, perished. Never before or since has such a destructive hurricane struck a major American city.

When the twenty-foot tide began to ebb, it carried with it not only the debris of buildings, trees, vehicles, and personal effects, but also the bodies of those who had perished in the storm and the disentombed—for complete graveyards were swept out to sea—including the cemetery where Charles Francis Coghlan's body had been interred.

Caskets that weren't shattered or sunk by the raging waters eventually ended up on the beaches or mangrove swamps bordering the Gulf of Mexico and the western Caribbean. Many sank. Most were never found. Others drifted for years over the seas. It is very possible that the "fleet" of coffins sighted by the crew of the *Sky Plover* in 1906 began their voyage in Galveston during the great hurricane. The schooner's captain mentioned in his log that there was at least several years of marine growth on the caskets. Why those coffins didn't drift apart in separate directions after six years is one of the many unexplained mysteries of the sea.

In October 1908, the same year that the *Sky Plover* vanished without a trace in an area that decades later would be called the Devil's Triangle, the first of the winter gales subsided that had swept the North Atlantic coast. Fishing vessels that had been forced to remain in port for over a week began putting out to sea. Throughout the Gulf of Saint Lawrence, they were busily setting their nets, trying to make up for the time lost the previous week. One group of boats working off Prince Edward Island came upon a waterlogged oblong box. Completely encrusted in barnacles, it was barely visible because of the waves washing over it. Having no idea what it was, but realizing that it must have some significance, the fishermen secured it to the stern of one of their boats and finished placing their nets. After the nets were set, they towed their "prize" ashore.

After they scraped away most of the marine growth, they realized that it was a coffin containing human remains. Cleaning off the remaining barnacles, they discovered a silver plate secured to the casket. The engraving on the plaque read, "Charles Francis Coghlan . . . born 1841, Prince Edward Island, Canada. Died 1899, Galveston, Texas."

TEN

A Possible Impossibility

One could reasonably call the yacht *Connemara IV* as being a kind of ghost ship. Even the most ardent skeptic would have to admit that the happenings associated with this yacht were more than merely strange. Real life science fiction? True life fantasy? A possible impossibility? You decide.

The strange last voyage of the motor yacht *Connemara IV* is one of the strangest hurricane mysteries ever in the West Indies. She was found crewless and adrift, but still shipshape, some four hundred miles southwest of Bermuda in September 1955. There was, however, no clue as to the fate of the crew. The large yacht, though somewhat battered, remained afloat and sound. During the second week in August, with winds up to 100 miles per hour, Hurricane Connie passed over the *Connemara IV*'s track from New York to where she was discovered. Less than a week later, Hurricane Diane, with its 125-mile-per-hour winds, roared over the same area and claimed more than two hundred lives. But there was more to come for the *Connemara IV*. Within two weeks, Hurricane Ione battered the identical sector of the Atlantic Ocean with its 125 mile-per-hour winds.

One can only comprehend the ferocity of a hurricane at sea by living through the experience. Most blue-water sailors agree that for the crew of a yacht to have remained at sea continuously for a month and to be belted by three hurricanes during that period would be almost beyond human endurance. But to survive one storm and to have another strike even before the waves of the first have diminished, and then to have yet a third slam in is almost unthinkable. The real mystery about the yacht *Connemara IV* is: how did she manage to survive three consecutive hurricanes while at sea?

Sounds incredible, doesn't it? I thought so, until I received a letter from Mr. J. E. Challenor of Barbados. With Mr. Challenor's permission, I am quoting part of his letter, for it throws an entirely new light on the strange saga of the *Connemara IV*.

"On September 22, 1955, at three o'clock in the morning, residents of Barbados were advised that a hurricane had been located east of the island. It was on a course that would pose a threat. As a result of this warning, all residents prepared for the worst. Supermarkets were opened, as well as hardware stores, and people began to board up their buildings. At seven o'clock in the morning, Hurricane Advisory Service stated that the hurricane would pass over the northern end of the island at about 9:00 A.M.

"The *Connemara IV* was a seventy-five-foot hardchine ex-RAF air-sea rescue launch which had been purchased as surplus after World War II by the late Mr. A. D. A. Cottingham in England, and was shipped on deck to Barbados to be used as a pleasure yacht. The original high-speed gasoline engines had been removed and she was re-engined with two war surplus AEC tank engines of about 150 horsepower each. Her speed with the new engines running free and light, with a clean bottom, was about ten knots.

"On the morning of September 22, *Connemara IV* was lying to a heavy mooring in the open roadstead of Carlisle Bay. Because of the approaching hurricane, the owner strengthened the mooring ropes and put out two additional anchors. There was little else he could do, as the exposed mooring was the only available anchorage.

"Instead of the hurricane passing north of the island, it veered southward and passed ten to fifteen miles off the southern coast at about 11:00 A.M. Winds of great velocity were experienced for about two and a half hours. The anemometer at Seawell International Airport registered 120 miles per hour. The hurricane was small but intense and, peculiarly, it was not accompanied by torrential rain. All the population took cover, and visibility was reduced to a few yards due to the driving sea spray. By midday the storm has passed. The hurricane eventually blew itself out over British Honduras.

"In Carlisle Bay, the sea in the wake of Hurricane Janet was awe-inspiring and dangerous. The owner of *Connemara IV* observed that she had disappeared. An investigation revealed that she had dragged her moorings and gone to sea.

"Two days later, on September 24, the sea was like glass, and I personally set out in a private aircraft to search for the missing yacht. The visibility was so good that from a height of six thousand feet, the whole string of islands from the Grenadines north as far as Dominica was clearly seen. There was no sign of the drifting yacht.

"Some days later the owner of the *Connemara IV* received a report from the owner of a tanker called the *Olympic Cloud* to the effect that he had spotted a large motor yacht adrift about thirty miles east of the island of St. Lucia and had taken her in tow for his designation—Dakar, West Africa. A subsequent report from the ship some days later stated that he had lost the tow during the night in the area of the Devil's Triangle. He believed that the stem of the *Connemara IV* had pulled out and the vessel sunk.

"I am in the firm belief that the vessel you mentioned in your book [*The Devil's Triangle*] is *Connemara IV*, from Barbados, which was registered in London and was a member of the 'Little Ship Club.' The only thing that perplexes me is that you state that the vessel was registered in New York. Could it have been that she was found by someone else, reregistered, and then lost again? I would be most interested to hear your comment on this information."

In reply to Mr. Challenor's letter, there are several comments to make concerning my first version of the story of the *Connemara IV* in my book *The Devil's Triangle*. I accept as fact now that the *Connemara IV* in my story was the same one referred to by Mr. Challenor. Thus, its hailing port was London, not New York. It can no longer be considered a "ghost ship," for there was no crew aboard her from the time she was last seen at Barbados before the storm until she was found three hurricanes later. That she was found thirty miles east of the island of St. Lucia is probably correct. It is not likely that she was found anywhere near Bermuda, as nearly every book and publication mentioning the incident has stated. If this popular version of the *Olympic Star* finding the yacht 150 miles southeast of Bermuda is correct, then we have what could be an even greater mystery.

Could the yacht *Connemara IV* drift almost 1,500 miles in four days from September 22, the day the storm hit, to September 26, the day she was found? To do so, she would have had to drift the distance through gale-force winds and storm-churned seas at a speed greater than her engines were able to manage through flat calm waters. Did some strange and possibly unearthly force move the *Connemara IV* that distance at one and a half times her running speed (fifteen knots)? Could there have been a crew of ghostly sailors aboard?

ELEVEN

The Great Wave of Death

Theories concerning strange events and disappearances at sea have varied from the practical, to the supernatural, to the preposterous. Various authors have even conjectured that giant spaceships or UFOs, larger than the Empire State Building, emerge from the deepest trenches of the ocean, breaking the surface with little or no disturbance of the water, and then prowl about in our atmosphere in search of humanoid victims.

Other writers have told of a giant solar-energized crystal nestled among the ruins of the "lost city of Atlantis" somewhere in the vicinity of the West Indies. Under certain conditions when a ship or plane passes in the vicinity, it is destroyed by rays or beams cast upward from this "ancient crystal." This submarine energy source is supposedly reposing far down, well beyond the furthest reach of the last glimmer of daylight. Those who believe this theory fail to explain how the crystal receives it solar energy when it is situated so far below the deepest reaches of the sun's rays.

Ancient mariners often returned home from extended sea voyages with tales of huge monsters and sea serpents that could devour whole ships along with their crews.

Clairvoyants have visualized great whirlpools resulting from undersea earthquakes, vortexes of such power that any surface vessel within a few miles of the "eye" or aircraft less than ten thousand feet above it would be sucked down into the depths of the sea. These oceanographic disturbances supposedly vanish as suddenly as they appear, leaving no traces of their victims nor any visible disturbance on the ocean's surface.

Some tell of flying saucers or other forms of spacecraft visiting earth from an alien planet and kidnapping ships, planes, mariners, airmen—and anyone else they might discover—and holding them captive in another dimension or a time warp.

In June 1969, a deposition hearing was held in New York concerning the mysterious disappearance of the sulfur ship *Marine Sulphur Queen*, a converted T-2 tanker. George H. Grant of Surf City, New Jersey, a seventy-two-year-old retired sea captain who spent nearly a half century at sea, suggested that a freak giant wave may have capsized the five-hundred-foot vessel and sent her to the bottom. Both the court and the press scoffed at the old captain's theory.

One may be skeptical about these conjectures, but are they all beyond credibility? It is a proven fact that far down in the deepest depths of the ocean, thousands of feet below those last traces of daylight, there exist giant creatures that are beyond description such as the giant squid. Their existence is without doubt, but their destructive capabilities are unknown.

Spaceships, UFOs, and flying saucers have been written and rewritten about countless times. But what about Captain Grant's "freak giant wave" theory? Freak giant wave are not tidal waves or tsunamis such as those that occasionally strike Hawaii and other Pacific islands— waves that result from submarine earthquakes that are recorded seismographically. Rather, they are huge waves from unknown causes occurring during supposedly normal conditions. Captain Grant may well have been wrong about the fate of the *Marine Sulphur Queen*, but his "freak giant wave" theory was far from erroneous.

October 21, 1962, was the fiftieth wedding anniversary of Anthony and Emma Hessler of Fort Lauderdale. To celebrate, they took a three-day cruise aboard the old SS *Florida*. The big white cruise ship put to sea from Miami at about 5:15 P.M. on Friday, October 19. Holding hands, the Hesslers stood at the rail on the promenade deck, looking back at the vessel's wake and the Miami skyline silhouetted by the late afternoon sun. The sky was cloudless. The sea was flat calm. The only wind was created by the ship's movement. At approximately seven o'clock the Hesslers sat down at their table in the dining room for their evening meal.

They had just been served their soup and salad when suddenly Emma Hessler found herself sitting on the deck, covered with food. Trays, dishes, and food were flying across the dining room. Chairs, tables, and people were sliding across the deck. The ship had suddenly taken a forty-five degree list to port.

Then slowly, very slowly, the ship began to right herself. Another few degrees, and she might have gone right on over. As the vessel began to reach an even keel again, people started struggling to their feet. Fortunately, there were no serious injuries. The sea was still calm, there was no wind, and the sky above was clear. Later a crew member commented to Mrs. Hessler, "Never before have I seen anything like this in all my twenty years at sea. If the passengers had known how close the ship was to going all the way over, there would have been a real panic."

Those who had been out on deck at the time never saw the wave coming. "It was as though it were invisible," commented one passenger. A freak giant wave covers such a vast area of water that, unlike a tidal wave crashing ashore, it is almost invisible from aboard a vessel at sea.

One of the greatest and most mysterious giant freak waves recorded in the Western Hemisphere occurred on August 29, 1916. The armored cruiser USS *Memphis* (converted from the old battleship *Tennessee*) and the gunboat USS *Castine* were riding at anchor at Santo Domingo harbor on the southern coast of the Dominican Republic. The sky was cloudless, the air was still, and the sea was flat. It was a typical hot and humid summer day around the island of Hispaniola, which is known as the Pearl of the Antilles. The Dominican Republic, one of the most prosperous countries in the Caribbean, occupies the eastern part of the island. The western half of the island is occupied by Haiti, one of the poorest West Indian countries if not the poorest.

Santo Domingo, among the first cities founded in the New World, straddles the Ozama River. Christopher Columbus's remains are reputed to be lying in one of that city's cathedrals. The river provides an excellent port for smaller vessels, but larger vessels have to ride at anchor in the open roadstead offshore. The reef-lined shore is

bordered by forty-foot-high bluffs. The roadstead aver-
ages ten fathoms in depth for approximately one mile
offshore, where the bottom drops straight down to one
hundred fathoms. Overlooking the anchorage is an ancient Spanish citadel, Fort Ozama.

In 1916, Fort Ozama was occupied by a detachment
of United States Marines, protecting American interests
in the unsettled political conditions on the island. The
Memphis had transported an additional contingent of
marines to reinforce those already established on the island. They were to maintain peace and see that the new
administration was honest. The cruiser, along with the
Castine, was standing by to provide additional support.

The sea that day was calm until about noon, when a
very slight swell began to roll in from the south. This
was a normal afternoon occurrence in these waters. Two
boatloads of sailors were sent ashore from the *Memphis*
as part of a recreation party—baseball and beer. The
commanding officer of the *Castine*, Commander Kenneth Bennett, went aboard the *Memphis* to lunch with
the cruiser's skipper, Captain Edward L. Beach, and then
to have some dental work done.

The eighteen-thousand-ton *Memphis* was held on an
east-northeast heading by seventy fathoms of anchor
chain. Six hundred yards inshore of the five-hundred-
foot-cruiser lay the twelve-hundred-ton *Castine*, also on
an east-northeast heading. Although the *Memphis* had
sixteen boilers, only two were in use for auxiliary power;
four others were kept ready for immediate firing. Captain Beach requested permission to fire up six other
boilers due to the exposed position of the anchorage, but
Rear Admiral Charles F. Pond, his superior, refused the
request in order to conserve coal.

As the afternoon wore on, the height of the waves seemed to be increasing; they were beginning to break over the bar at the mouth of the river. Out where the vessels were straining at their anchors, the waves were unnoticeable. The wind was minimal, and the sky remained cloudless. Those aboard the vessels thought nothing of their ships' gentle rolling, which was normal for vessels at anchor in an open roadstead. The sea surface was smooth, with hardly a ripple. The swells were increasing, however, but so slowly that they were barely discernible. The two captains finally became aware that the *Memphis* was rolling a bit more quickly than before. Shoreward, they noticed that the *Castine*'s rolling was also increasing. A boat was readied, and Captain Bennett returned to his ship.

Surf was building up along the shoreline. The ships were rolling faster. The *Memphis*'s number two motor launch was ordered ashore to pick up half of the recreation party. With each minute, the ship's movements increased. Still, the sea appeared calm and smooth.

One boat from the *Castine* and two from the *Memphis* were circling their mother ships, but the two ships were rolling so much that hoisting the boats aboard would have been too hazardous. Still, there was no wind, and the sea was still. Additional boilers were ordered fired up on both ships.

Captain Beach and his executive officer, Lieutenant Commander Yancey Williams, looked down from the bridge of the *Memphis* at the smooth sea with its invisible waves, then up at the mastheads as they gestured a sweeping arc across the clear blue sky. They could see the breaker line moving farther out from shore, almost to where the *Castine* lay at anchor. Black smoke belched from the gunboat's stack. Her boilers had been fired up, and she was about to get under way. Captain Beach felt William's hand on his shoulder. He took his eyes from the gunboat and looked out to sea.

Deep down in the cruiser's engine room, the machinists were waiting for the head of steam pressure that would enable them to crank over the main engines. All nonessential machinery was shut down to conserve steam pressure.

There were problems in the fire rooms where men stripped to the waist were struggling to get additional boilers lit. A number of steel floor plates had been removed to facilitate the painting of the bilges. Men were laboring to get them back in place and bolted down. The fireboxes beneath the boilers were usually lit by mixing hot coals from the already operating fireboxes with coal spread out on the gratings. Coal passers were struggling across the heaving fire-room floors, working their way around the openings where the floor plates had yet to be replaced. At times, the heave of the ship would cause a bucket of red-hot coals to pitch out of a man's hands, causing its contents to mix with the fresh coal spilling from the bunkers.

The ship was rolling so hard that the water tenders were having difficulty maintaining the right water level in the boilers. The men in the fire room had worked under rough sea conditions many times, but always when the ship was under way. When a ship is at anchor, its rolling motion is very different from when it is moving through the water.

Looking seaward across the deceptively placid waters, Captain Beach could see no horizon. He and Williams stared horror-stricken at where the horizon should have been. All they could see was a wall of foamy yellow water nearly a hundred feet in height.

It was 3:45 P.M. Calls of "Secure for heavy weather!" "All hands, man your stations!" and "Batten the gun ports!" echoed through the *Memphis*.

The breaker line had moved farther out from shore. The *Castine*, smoke pouring from her stack, was periodically engulfed in the surf. Waves were breaking over her decks. Her crew was engaged in a life-and-death battle to hoist her anchor. Just a short distance out, the sea appeared smooth.

The *Memphis*'s liberty boat, which a few minutes earlier had entered the mouth of the Ozama River through calm water en route to the recreation area, was now outward bound with half the liberty party. Another launch was to have been sent ashore for the other half of the party. The entrance to the river had transformed from a proverbial "mill pond" to a "tempest in a teapot." The launch and its thirty-one men were caught in the wild surf. Coxswain Bill Smith was unable to bring the boat about and return to the safety of the river. The laboring engine could barely maintain the necessary forward motion of the launch. Those aboard anticipated smoother waters once the boat cleared the mouth of the river.

Far down beneath the *Memphis*'s waterline, life for the men fighting to light additional boilers had become a nightmare of hissing steam, bouncing floor plates, hot rolling coals underfoot, shovels and pokers flying through the air, screams from the voice tube to the bridge begging for steam, and seawater pouring through the air vents.

Waves were crashing over the ship's superstructure, forcing tons of water down the ventilators leading to the engine and fire rooms. The ship was rolling more than forty-five degrees. Men were grabbing anything that offered a solid handhold. The sailors in the bridge were awestruck as they stared at the huge yellow wall of water. It was only a mile away. Still, the sky above was clear; there was little or no wind. The water next to the *Memphis*'s hull was incredibly calm.

Aboard the *Castine*, conditions were the same, except that the gunboat had steam to her engines. The propellers were turning to take some of the strain off her anchor chain. At the fo'c'sle, the men on the anchor detail were encountering difficulties in raising the anchor. The clutch in the capstan was slipping. The bow would raise clear out of the water, then drop thirty feet back down. With each plunge, those working on the anchor capstan were in a state of weightlessness. Captain Bennett yelled repeatedly through his speaking tube, "Up anchor! Fo'c'sle, heave up the anchor!"

"Aye, aye!" was the reply from the bow. But still they couldn't get the capstan working. Each roll of the ship was heavier than the one before. The only movement of air was caused by the ship's gyration.

Aboard the *Memphis*'s motor launch, Coxswain Smith stared ahead at a breaker higher than any yet encountered. It was too late to turn back. The general feeling of those aboard was that if they could make it over this wave, they'd be in the clear. The launch climbed up the nearly vertical wall of the approaching wave. But ahead loomed a second oncoming wave, even higher and steeper than the previous one. And once again the launch climbed up and over the comber. Then came a third and a fourth—each wave bigger than the previous one. The fifth breaker engulfed the boat, half filling it with water.

The engine, its ignition flooded, sputtered and stopped. As the launch's engineer, Fireman E. J. Drager, vainly attempted to restart the motor, others were frantically bailing with buckets, caps, or anything else that would hold water. All forward movement ceased. The launch broached and lay abeam to the next breaking sea, which filled the boat. The weight of the engine pulled the boat down, stern first, from under the men. Suddenly, thirty-one heads were bobbing in the water.

Captain Beach was still calling down to the fire room for steam as the yellow wall of water engulfed the *Memphis*. The men had just fired up two more boilers when a deluge of water came cascading down the stacks, drowning out the fires. The men fought to keep the original two fires going. So extreme was the motion of the ship that with each roll her four stacks were scooping in seawater.

Shortly before 4:00 P.M., the *Castine*'s anchor windlass was operating, and the anchor was being hoisted. Before the gunboat could make headway, however, she began drifting down upon the men from the *Memphis*'s launch struggling in the water. As the *Castine* neared the swimming sailors, men lining the rails began throwing life jackets, locker doors, tabletops, and anything else that would float to the men in the water. But so extreme was the rolling and pitching of the *Castine* that Commander Bennett, concerned about the possibility of his ship plunging down upon the swimmers, ordered the vessel away from the men. The *Castine* headed out to sea—climbing over the huge yellow wave.

The three motor launches—one from the *Castine* and two from the *Memphis*—had been ordered to "lie to" after it was decided that sea conditions were too rough for them to be hoisted aboard their ships. Although the waves that tossed the two ships about were virtually unnoticeable from the launches, the ships were ordered to head farther out to sea from the anchorage and wait for the *Castine* to pick them up.

The officers on the *Memphis*'s bridge were praying for steam. Most of the crew not working the ship were gathered on the boat deck. Objects, including the ship's piano, that had broken loose from their lashings were sliding back and forth across the decks. Those who got in the way never knew what hit them. A boat broke loose. Two men trying to secure it were carried over the side with it.

The engine-room crew was still standing by for steam that would never come. The men in the fire rooms were fighting a losing battle. Rupturing steam lines were adding to their problems. What little steam they had was escaping. Maintaining steam to the pumps was more urgent than getting steam to the engines. Periodically, the ship's power would fail momentarily. Still, the fire-room gang struggled on, the red glow from the furnace doors and those electric lanterns that hadn't been smashed providing the only illumination.

Everyone aboard felt the *Memphis* shudder. The ship's keel had bounced against the bottom halfway through a roll. Again and again, the cruiser's bottom struck the coral sea floor. Hull plates were bulging inward. Water and steam lines began rupturing. Clouds of steam engulfed the fire and engine rooms.

The USS *Memphis* drew less than thirty feet of water. Yet she was striking the bottom in fifty-five feet of water. The invisible waves had become visible. Lifeboats were being smashed. Waves were higher than the cruiser's stacks. Men were being washed overboard. The ship's anchor was dragging, and she was moving closer to shore.

In a last desperate attempt to save the ship, the anchor chain was cast free, and the little steam available was applied to the engines. The huge reciprocating engines began to turn over, and the twenty-six-foot-diameter propellers started to churn. But the ship came to life only momentarily. Before the *Memphis* could gain way, the steam pressure dropped. The giant propellers, which had pushed the ship's hull nearly 180,000 miles through the waters of the world since 1906, stopped forever.

The engine and fire rooms became a nightmare for those who had been struggling to get the ship moving. Some were scalded by steam blasting from broken pipes. Others were slashed by unidentified objects hurling across the darkened spaces. Men were scorched as their bodies slammed into hot steam lines and machinery. Quarter-inch-thick steel floor plates were bending like playing cards. The ship's bottom, grinding against the coral, echoed like the sound of screaming voices. The USS *Memphis* was dying.

Topside, only a light, gentle breeze was blowing. The tropical sun was beating down on the anchorage. But the sea no longer appeared tranquil. The 18,000-ton cruiser's bow heaved completely out of the water, exposing nearly a third of the *Memphis*'s keel. Her four stacks were still scooping in water with each roll. The seas continued to push the overwhelmed ship broadside, toward the rock-strewn shore. Wave after wave swept across her decks.

Lining the forty-foot bluffs were marines, members of the cruiser's recreation party who didn't attempt to return to the ship, and thousands of Dominicans. National and political differences were forgotten for the moment. All were preparing for the rescue of the men aboard the *Memphis*. No one knew whether the ship would smash to pieces on the rocks or roll over, dumping the crew into the pounding seas. Although the rescuers were waiting atop the bluff, forty feet above the maelstrom, they were still being drenched by seawater—not spray, but solid seawater. Vehicles were lining up in preparation to take the survivors, if any, to hospitals being set up in churches and other large buildings.

With each successive wave, the *Memphis* crashed shoreward. With each roll, as she careened wildly from beam to beam, it appeared that she would not right herself. Yet she continued to defy gravity and recover from the roll.

Both those aboard the vessel and those ashore knew that it was no longer a matter of saving the ship, but rather of saving the men aboard. With each successive thundering wave, the ship moved closer to the coral cliffs. As each wave receded, it left the vessel high and dry, as though she were in drydock, momentarily. As she was engulfed by the next incoming wave, she would rise off the bottom and continue her crashing journey shoreward.

Out at sea, the *Castine* did not find the smoother waters her captain had expected. Although the waves were no longer breaking, they were high and steep, burying the gunboat's rails with each roll. Waves were higher than ever seen by most of the crew. Still, the sun shone, and the wind was minimal.

It was shortly before 5:00 P.M. when the USS *Memphis* smashed onto the coral ocean floor, never to rise again—a mere hundred feet from the bluff. Although a large portion of her bottom was ripped away, she remained upright. Lifelines were immediately established between the ship and those on the bluff. The dead and wounded were removed first, then the crew. As Captain Beach, the last man to leave the ship, set foot on land, a wind-driven rain engulfed the dead ship.

The three motor launches, concerned that the *Castine* would not be able to locate them in the dark, set course for a lighthouse just up the coast from Santo Domingo at approximately 8:00 P.M., but their fate was already sealed. The *Memphis*'s number-three boat got to within a mile of shore when she was swamped, drowning two of the four men aboard her. The cruiser's other boat made it to the shore just west of the lighthouse, but three of the seven sailors aboard it were battered to death when the boat crashed onto the rocks. The *Castine*'s motor launch with its crew of three was never seen again.

The heavily damaged *Castine* limped back to Santo Domingo harbor the following day. The *Memphis*, which from a distance appeared to be a proud naval vessel riding at anchor, was solidly aground next to the bluff. Close up, she was a battered hulk, her bottom ripped out. The onetime pride of the fleet would rest where she died for many years before being dismantled for scrap. As a result of the great wave of death, forty-six men died and scores were injured. Captain Beach was later exonerated from any fault in the loss of his ship.

From whence the great wave of death came was a subject of controversy aboard naval vessels for years to come. Some attributed it to a submarine earthquake or undersea volcanic eruption. Others blamed a tropical weather disturbance hundreds of miles to the south. But it was never definitely ascertained where the huge yellow wave originated.

There is more to tell, for even after the sea subsided and all survivors were established safely ashore, mysterious events occurred aboard the dead ship. Stories of one incident in particular were told aboard naval vessels from the Yangtze River to the North Atlantic.

Several days after the storm, part of the salvage crew began bringing ashore food and other supplies from the ship. Two men, wading through knee-deep water in one of the lower decks, their eyes not yet used to the darkened space, heard what sounded like someone groaning. Turning up the flame in their kerosene lantern, they looked around the dimly lit compartment but saw nothing. Yet, the sound came from all directions. Then, with a feeling of relief, they realized that they were hearing the sounds of straining metal in the ship's hull. Although they could not see or feel any movement, the ship was shifting just enough to put stress on her frames and plating, thus creating the weird, groaning sounds.

The two men moved over to a hatch, opened it, and entered the next darkened compartment. As the light from the lantern cast its dim glow over part of the room, they saw something move just beyond the range of its beam. Lifting the lantern higher, they sloshed on ahead, but after a step or two they froze. A spectral figure, its face familiar but ashen and sullen, stared back at the two men, then turned and disappeared into the darkness. Before the dropped lantern struck the water, the two sailors were already splashing their way out of the compartment.

Their shipmates scoffed when the two men told what

they had experienced below decks—until other members of the crew had similar experiences. Some reported seeing two apparitions. The part of the ship that was above water was searched thoroughly, but no one, human or otherwise, was found. However, those who saw the figures in the darkened areas below decks agreed that they resembled two of the *Memphis*'s missing crew members—named Teshack and Dugan—who were believed to have perished when the ship's liberty launch foundered in the breaking waves at the mouth of the Ozama River.

Eventually, the men of the *Memphis* were assigned to other ships in the fleet or to bases ashore. And whenever old shipmates from the cruiser gathered at reunions during the years that followed, the talk of their old ship would eventually turn to the "ghosts of the *Memphis*." Every once in a while, however, a sailor would turn up and swear that he had seen the likes of Teshack and Dugan at a waterfront bar in some remote part of the world. Could the two crewmen have survived the tragic boat ride into the wild surf? Is it possible they, too, were aboard the ship seeking supplies? Could they have deserted with the help of sympathetic Dominicans who were hostile toward the United States government? This could well have been the case—or perhaps Dugan and Teshack really did return from their watery graves.

TWELVE

The Ghost Ship

Reconnaissance photos identified it as being American. Aerial observers swore that it was a United States Navy ship. Submarine commanders spared her. "Impossible. Impossible," came the reply from Naval Intelligence at Pearl Harbor. "All of our destroyers are accounted for!"

Yet continued sightings of an American destroyer sailing far behind Japanese lines created one of the most bizarre controversies in the Pacific War Zone.

The subject was a U.S. Navy World War I class of destroyer, a "four piper" (four stacks), many of which were still being used during the Second World War. The photographs and descriptions indicated that the ship could be nothing else. But what ship was it? What was it doing so deep in enemy territory? Was it on some secret mission? Furthermore, every American destroyer was accounted for, and none had been assigned to such an impossible mission. Fleet commanders were baffled.

A number of old "four pipers" had been converted to

destroyer minesweepers (DMSs), fast minesweepers (DMs) and attack transports (APDs). Again, Fleet Headquarters was contacted. "Are any converted APD, DMS, or DM destroyers unaccounted for?" Again, the reply was negative. Still, reported sightings of the ghost destroyer poured in. The spectral silhouette of this United States destroyer would materialize out of the blue, her existence completely indisputable to those American airmen and submariners who sighted her. She was the perfect phantasmal apparition. Or was she?

Thinking the mystery ship might really be an American destroyer on a top-secret mission, Headquarters spared the vessel from American bombs and torpedos. Then, suddenly, reports of the enigmatic United States warship stopped coming in. Where was she? What happened to her? Had the Japanese sunk her?

It wasn't until after Hiroshima and Nagasaki were bombed and the Japanese had surrendered that the mystery of the United States Navy's "ghost ship" was solved.

On October 15, 1945, two months after the war ended, American forces inspecting the Japanese navy base in the Kure-Hiroshima area, deep in the heart of the enemy's homeland, found a cluster of Japanese destroyers rafted together out in the harbor. In the middle of the group was the Japanese ship *Patrol Vessel 102*. But *Patrol Vessel 102* had the lines and nomenclature of an American Navy four-stack destroyer. Although her stacks had been modified and a tripod mast fitted to the hull, she was unequivocally "made in the USA." Why was this American Navy destroyer serving in the Japanese fleet? The answer goes back to the early days of World War II when the United States was the losing side and the Japanese, almost unchallenged, had been sinking too many Allied ships.

During these months immediately followng the Japanese attack on Pearl Harbor, the waters around Java, Borneo, Timor, Balikpapan, Celebes, Sumatra, Bali and other places near where the South China Sea meets the Pacific Ocean, saw some of the most desperate and bloody sea battles of World War II. Against superior numbers and newer and better armed ships, the iron men and the iron ships of the American, British, Dutch and Australian Navies jolted the hell out of the Japanese navy. However, that phase of the war proved victorious for the ships of Japan. Yet while the Japanese were enjoying the "dinner," the Allied sailors were getting some of the appetizer and dessert.

Among those Allied fighting ships was DesRon (Destroyer Squadron) 29 of the United States Asiatic Fleet. This little "tin can" force made a heroic attempt to arrest the rampage of nearly the entire Japanese Navy during those hectic early months of the war. They did it without supplies, without bases, and—worst of all—without air support. They proved to be a constant thorn in the sides of the enemy ships. Without this resistance by the Allied Asiatic Fleet, say some historians, the Japanese might have followed up on their Pearl Harbor attack with an earlier assault against Midway Island—before the Americans were ready to repel them. Or they might have succeeded with another onslaught against the Hawaiian Islands.

During the night of February 17, 1942, the Dutch cruiser *Tromp*, accompanied by four old American destroyers, the *Parrott*, the *Edwards*, the *Pilsbury*, and the

Stewart—all steaming at twenty-five knots—entered the Badoeng Strait. One minute later, they opened fire on a flotilla of Japanese destroyers and transports. Although the allied ships failed to halt or delay the invasion, they did inflict damage upon the Japanese. And they all managed to escape, but *Tromp* suffered severe damage, and *Stewart* was disabled.

With emergency repairs, *Stewart* managed to reach Soerabaja, a seaport where there was still an undamaged dry dock that could handle the ship. It was Sunday. The *Stewart* was floated into the dry dock and steadied with blocks and beams. With pumps draining the dock's ballast compartments, the old destroyer began to rise out of the water. Then, the ineptness of the Dutch and native workmen accomplished what the Japanese couldn't do. Panicked by constant enemy air attacks and being forced to work on the Sabbath, the workers incorrectly shored up the *Stewart*. As the dry dock rose higher out of the water, the destroyer tilted over with her port side jammed against the side of the dry dock. Before she could be righted and refloated, enemy aircraft swept down on Soerabaja. The damage was devastating. Most of the dock area had been leveled. One bomb struck the *Stewart*, but the damage was not beyond repair. A Dutch destroyer and submarine docked in the harbor were sunk during the attack. The surviving ships, American and Dutch, put to sea. The disabled *Stewart* was left behind. There was no way that she could have been repaired before the Japanese forces arrived.

On March 2, 1942, to prevent the destroyer from falling into enemy hands, her crew rigged her with heavy explosives. Then, satisfied that the explosives were ready, the demolitionists set the timing mechanisms and fled Soerabaja. The *Stewart* would never go to sea again. Or so they thought.

Either the explosives failed to go off or Japanese sympathizers among the natives disarmed them. Thus, unbeknown to the Americans, Japanese workmen repaired the *Stewart*, renamed her *Patrol Vessel 102* and sailed her to Japan where she was outfitted for service with the Japanese Navy. The spectral ship was not a ghostly destroyer after all.

On October 28, 1945, the old destroyer was manned by an American prize crew and renamed *DD 242*. She could not be renamed *Stewart*. Having thought her destroyed, the Navy struck her from the Register and named a new destroyer escort (DE 238) the USS *Stewart*. On November 3, 1945, the USS *DD 242*, her boilers fired up, cast off for the United States.

THIRTEEN

The Coast Guard's Encounters with the Bizarre

F og has always been associated with mystery in both film and literature; the more supernatural the mystery, the more fog. People have a natural fear of the unknown. We are not afraid of the fog itself. We are afraid of what it hides. There have been disastrous maritime, aviation, and highway tragedies attributed directly to fog. It is easy for the reader to sit in his armchair snuggled in the security of his living room and deny any fear of fog. But unless you've attempted landing an airplane or taking a vessel into port without radar, you are really unaware of the eeriness of fog. Driving slowly down a fog-engulfed expressway is nothing in comparison.

In October 1954, the Coast Guard buoy tender *Smilax* was proceeding north from Brunswick, Georgia, to various points along the South Carolina coast where she was to repair or replace buoys and other navigational aids that had been damaged or destroyed by Hurricane Hazel several days earlier. Winds of 150 miles per hour

Of all the seas and oceans on earth, the North Atlantic is the most unforgiving.

(U.S. Shipping Board photo)

The USS *Nina* had one of the longest careers in the U.S. Navy. After forty-five years of yeoman service, the tug put to sea from Norfolk, VA, on February 6, 1910, was never to be seen again.

(U.S. Navy photo)

The U.S. Navy was very concerned with the loss of the tugboat *Conestoga,* seen here at the San Diego Navy Yard shortly before she sailed off into oblivion.

(U.S. Navy photo)

The only trace remaining of the ill-fated SS Marine *Sulphur Queen* was the vessel's trailboard, which had been affixed to the ship's bridge.

(*Miami News*)

Two doomed ships —the USS *Cyclops* coaling the USS *Memphis* (formerly the *Tennessee*) at sea. Within a few years, the *Memphis* would be destroyed by a mysterious freak wave, and the *Cyclops* vanished without a trace.

(U.S. Navy photo)

The last picture of the USS *Cyclops* taken by the last crewman to leave the ship before she met her strange fate.

(Conrad H. Nervig)

Lieutenant Conrad Nervig, the last crewman to escape the *Cyclops*.

(Conrad H. Nervig)

Conrad Nervig fifty years later with a model of the doomed USS *Cyclops*. Days after the deck officer left the ship, it became one of the greatest mysteries of the sea.

(Richard Winer)

On September 8, 1923, U.S. Navy destroyers became entrapped and destroyed in the mysterious fangs of the Devil's Jaw near Santa Barbara, CA.

(Admiral William V. Pratt)

The ghosts that once haunted Great Isaac Rock in the Bahamas were long gone on Christmas week of 1967 when two lighthouse keepers simply vanished without a trace.

(Bahamas News Bureau)

Waterspouts, tornadoes at sea, are beautiful . . . until you sail into one.

(U.S. Coast Guard)

had slammed ashore along the Carolina coast at 9:00 A.M. on October 15. Ninety-eight lives were lost in the United States and Canada alone. Property damage was in excess of $251,600.

As the hundred-foot-long *Smilax* crossed Ossabaw Sound near Savannah, she ran into a very dense fog. Seaman Second Class Ike Levine, later a master chief boatswain's mate at the Fort Lauderdale Coast Guard Station and now retired, took over the bow watch just before midnight. Once each minute, the vessel's foghorn bellowed out a five-second blast as the *Smilax* felt her way through the mist at a speed of under two knots.

From ahead came the sound of another foghorn. With each blast, the source of the sound seemed to be getting closer. Chief Warrant Officer Creech, in command of the buoy tender, brought his ship to a stop. The sound of the foghorn ahead continued to blast through the fog but came no closer. Thinking that the other vessel had also stopped, Creech waited. The sound of the other horn came no closer. Creech ordered the *Smilax* to move slowly ahead. The radar in the bridge showed no other vessel in the vicinity.

A minute later the foghorn of the ship that wasn't there blared from astern. Still the radar screen indicated no other vessel in any direction. Then Levine thought that he heard the foghorn of another ship ahead somewhere. The radar showed nothing but the shoreline and a buoy. The seaman tightened his grip on the cold, wet bow rail. Again, he heard a foghorn from somewhere in the fog ahead. The first horn was getting lower, as though drifting or moving further astern. The new horn seemed to be getting louder, yet the radar continued to show only the shoreline and the buoy.

Once more Creech stopped the *Smilax*. The coast guard vessel drifted slowly ahead with the current. Creech ordered Levine to turn on the carbon arc searchlight. As the seaman was plugging in the connector for the carbon arc light, the men on the *Smilax* heard still another foghorn from somewhere else ahead, but, as before, the radar gave no indication of any ship or boat within its range.

The searchlight penetrated only a short distance into the fog. Then, suddenly from above, a beam of light came shining down on the *Smilax*. The beam moved from just ahead of the ship to directly over it. There was no aircraft above the vessel. The night was dead still except for the eerie foghorns and the *Smilax*'s own whistle. Levine tilted his searchlight straight up at the other light; the other light went out. As Levine turned his light back down toward the water, the buoy tender emerged from the fog.

The night ahead was clear, and there were no other craft in sight. Still, the men of the Smilax could hear the strange foghorns. Then, the crew solved the mystery. Each of the various fish-packing and ice houses along shore had its own foghorn; to the average person, they all sounded alike or similar, but to the fishermen who used those facilities, each foghorn had a different sound. The horns were used to guide the fishermen to the particular ice houses they were seeking.

But what about the strange light that shone down on the *Smilax*? Where did it come from? Was it another mystery of the unknown? After much discussion, the crew concluded that it could only have originated from the coast guard vessel's own light. Under certain conditions, especially when there are various layers and densities, fog can refract a beam of light, bending its ray in several directions, including back toward its source. There have even been occurrences where a refracted beam has returned as a different color light.

Although the United States Coast Guard can usually offer some sort of logical explanation for many strange happenings at sea, their own vessels are not immune to the unexplainable.

The USCGC (United States Coast Guard Cutter) *Yamacraw* was a former World War II mine-layer converted by the Coast Guard to a combination cable-laying and research ship. She had a white superstructure and a black hull. The large letters on her hull disclosed her designation—WARC 333. The name *Yamacraw* was derived from a tribe of Florida Indians. Commander William D. Strauch, USCG, was captain of the 189-foot ship. Her normal complement was fifty-one.

On August 8, 1956, the *Yamacraw* was on a heading of 165 degrees. Her position was 30.65 north and 73.80 west, placing her in what is sometimes referred to as the Sargasso Sea, an area north and east of the Bahamas and approximately five hundred miles east of Jacksonville. It was 0130 hours when the radar operator called out, "Large land mass dead ahead: range, twenty-eight miles."

"Impossible!" responded Ensign Francis J. Flynn. "There's only one land mass on our heading and that's the Dominican Republic, over eight hundred miles away."

The radar operator adjusted and readjusted his equipment. Again, he called the officer of the watch. "Mr. Flynn, the radar is showing a land mass directly ahead on our course. Take a look for yourself."

Flynn studied the radar screen. "You're right, it's got to be a land mass. Look how straight it is . . . almost as if it were drawn by a pencil. Wake up the skipper. I'm going to check the compasses and take another position fix."

The sea was flat, smooth. The sky was clear. Every star and constellation that should have been visible in that area was in view. The compasses were correct, and the ensign's sightings tallied with his previous fix. Still, the radar screen showed a huge land mass directly ahead on the *Yamacraw*'s course. Steaming at twelve and a half knots, the ship had reduced the distance to twenty-four miles. "Maintain one hundred sixty-five degrees," ordered the captain.

Less than two hours later, those on the bridge were gazing ahead in awe. No more than a mile ahead, looming up out of the sea, was a huge, dark mass that seemed to stretch from horizon to horizon and reached skyward as high as the men could see. The radar, which was capable of penetrating fog, showed this to be a solid mass.

Minutes later, the *Yamacraw* was alongside the huge mass. Commander Strauch ordered his men to rig the thirty-six-inch-diameter carbon arc search light. As the ship idled along, parallel to the mass, the men noticed that it did not come up out of the water but rather started about a foot and a half to two feet above the sea's surface. The ship was less than fifty feet away when the big searchlight was turned on, yet its powerful beam penetrated no more than a few feet into the mass. The radar could not penetrate the mass at all. The light disclosed the mass's color as being a brownish gray.

For half an hour, the *Yamacraw* steamed slowly along

the edge of the mass. From time to time, the captain would order the ship to penetrate it for a minute or so at a time. There was no dampness or temperature change as there would have been in the case of fog. Then, the ship pulled several hundred yards away and continued steaming alongside the mass, which formed a straight line running northeast to southwest.

After a few minutes, Commander Strauch ordered the helm eased over to starboard, and the USCGC *Yama-craw* slowly eased back into the strange, brownish-gray fog that was impenetrable by either searchlight or radar.

The high-intensity carbon arc lamp became only a dull glow, and then was only visible when one looked directly at it. As before, there was no change in temperature or humidity. On deck, visibility was absolute zero. Some of the men groping their way around the *Yama-craw*'s deck commented that the substance into which they had steamed felt like suspended particles of fine sand or dust. Yet there was no movement of the mass, as there would have been if it were one of those rare dust storms at sea. The air was dead still. The ship moved forward with just enough way to maintain steerage. The radar screen showed only a green clutter. The ship's compasses still worked.

Suddenly, there was spontaneous coughing among the men who were out on deck. Their eyes began burning. It was as though the huge wall of fog contained an irritant of some kind.

"Engine room to bridge! Engine room to bridge!" came a call from below. "We're losing steam pressure! Something's affecting the combustion! The boilers ain't working right! Engine RPMs are falling off!"

With the reduced RPMs, the *Yamacraw*'s forward

movement was barely discernible. Men were having more difficulty breathing. A message reporting the ship's predicament was prepared for radio transmission. The captain was about to order the helmsman to bring the ship about in order to escape from the huge mass when the *Yamacraw* eased out of the mass.

"It's almost as though we sailed right through a solid wall," commented a seaman.

"It felt like we took the ship right through the gates of hell," responded another voice.

"Engine room to bridge. Steam pressure returning to normal. Commence desired speed," came the call from below.

It was nearly dawn. For another thirty minutes the Coast Guard ship steamed alongside the huge fog. The ship's radar was unable to detect the size of the mass. It seemed to stretch endlessly from northeast to southwest, and formed a perfect line both vertically and horizontally. Even as the first streaks of dawn began to penetrate the darkness, the men couldn't see the top of the fog.

Then, just as the sun began coming into view, the immense brownish-gray form vanished. The sea surface appeared normal where the mass had been. There was no dust or sediment on the ship, even though many of the crew had tasted dust in the air while the vessel was in the mass. The radar indicated nothing solid within range. The *Yamacraw* spent half a day cruising the area before continuing on, but found nothing to indicate what the strange thing had been.

Oceanographers were unable to discover what it was that the *Yamacraw* had voyaged through, nor could they even conjecture. There is no record of similar phenomenon.

Perhaps the *Yamacraw* was a very lucky ship, for no one can really say what might have happened to her had she not exited when she did. She too might have become part of the legendary chronicle of the Devil's Triangle.

The men of the navigation section of the coast guard cutter *Dilligence* wore "triangles" hanging from their necks as a jest after seeing the movie *The Devil's Triangle* in Key West, but according to Quartermaster First Class Vincent Hamborski they were totally unaware of anything happening to them or their ship on its next voyage. After all, the *Dilligence* had been operating almost exclusively in the Devil's Triangle for some time and had never been involved in anything unusual.

A month later, in November 1974, the *Dilligence* was racing through the night across the Straits of Florida to the scene of a burning cargo ship. Since the cutter was south of Cay Sal Banks, she received an order to abort the mission. The burning ship had been beached in Bahamian waters and was under that government's jurisdiction. The coast guard ship put about and headed back toward Key West.

Just west of the Cay Sal Banks, Radioman Third Class Kenneth Irvin suddenly lost all communication on the *Dilligence*'s single side-band radio. He switched to the continuous wave (Morse code transmitter) radio, but still there was no communication. The radio-teletype was also out of commission. Trying to maintain his cool, Irvin attempted to send a message with the AM transmitter, but that set, too, was not working.

As the officers on watch were contemplating what to

do about the *Dilligence*'s total loss of all communications, the lookouts reported that a green light was plummeting into the sea some distance off. Less than a minute later, another green light was seen falling into the sea. The helm was put over, and the vessel headed toward the sightings. At first, it was thought that the green lights might have been distress flares, but they were seen coming down only, and not going up.

It took about twenty minutes for the *Dilligence* to reach the estimated position of the falling lights. Nothing was found—only an empty sea. About that time, the radios began working again, and communications were once more established. A thorough examination of the equipment by the ship's radio technicians failed to disclose anything wrong with the radios.

Although rare, radio "dead spots" do occur in the area of the Atlantic Ocean referred to as the Devil's Triangle. When this happens, commercial and military craft usually are able to switch over to another frequency or wavelength and maintain communication. But for all communications systems to malfunction at the same time with no apparent cause is rather exceptional.

But what about the green lights seen by the lookouts aboard the *Dilligence*? Distress signal flares? Possibly, but no flares were seen going up, as is usually the case with distress signals. The ship's radar picked up nothing, and there was only an empty sea when the cutter reached the estimated location and began searching. There was mention of falling stars and meterorites. But the odds are virtually a million to one against two being seen at the same location within minutes of each other. It is quite possible the phenomena experienced by the *Dilligence* that night are explainable. However, the possibility also exists that what happened out there was something beyond our understanding.

The services of the United States Coast Guard are not limited to patrolling for smugglers and running in search and rescue operations. Among its operations are administrative and support sections based ashore, lighthouses and lightships, the marine inspection branch, weather stations, and the "working coast guard," as the men on the buoy tenders refer to themselves. The buoy tender *Hollyhock*, based at Miami Beach, is a ship of the "working coast guard."

I happened to be in Key West when the *Hollyhock* was working out of that city, maintaining and repairing aids to navigation. A rap session with that vessel's executive officer, Lieutenant Bill Wissman, led to even more information concerning strange happenings to vessels of the United States Coast Guard.

The *Hollyhock* had been working in Bahamian waters between New Providence and Andros Island where the United States Navy maintains its underwater test-and-evaluation center—sometimes referred to as AUTEC. The buoy tender was returning to Miami Beach one evening in August 1974. She had just cleared Great Isaac Lighthouse, which is the westernmost lighthouse in the Bahama Islands, and was entering the Straits of Florida when the radar man reported a land mass or island ten miles ahead—an area where there should have been only open sea. The Florida coastline was still almost fifty miles away. The only land between Florida and the Bahama Islands is Cay Sal Banks, over a hundred miles to the south. The image on the scope bore a strong resemblance to Andros Island, from whence the *Hollyhock* had just come, except it was smaller in size. The radar was checked and rechecked, but everything showed normal, except the image on the radar screen. As the ship ploughed on through the dark waters of the Gulf Stream, the mass remained on the radar scope, except that it appeared to be moving with the ship and maintaining its distance. It was too large to be another ship. The radar man continued checking and rechecking. Except for the land mass, everything else was normal. Great Isaac and the Biminis showed up astern to the east, just as they should have. The Florida mainland was yet out of range. Still, ahead was the land mass. Those on the bridge with their night glasses strained to see ahead, but ten miles was too far. The night was calm and clear. No matter what the men did, the radar continued to show an island where there shouldn't have been one.

When the coast of Florida came within range of the *Hollyhock*'s radar, it appeared normal, but the land mass remained. Finally, when the ship was within ten miles from the coast, the strange image on the radar scope began to blend in with the shoreline and gradually diminish. No one aboard the *Hollyhock* could offer any solution to the mystery. However, several radar-equipped yachts have reported picking up the image of a "ghost island" while voyaging across the Straits of Florida.

Three months later, the *Hollyhock* was returning to Miami Beach from San Juan. She was heading westward off the north coast of Haiti when all of her radios began to malfunction. All communications with other ships and shore bases ceased—with one exception. The ship was able to communicate with one station—the coast guard station at San Francisco, California. The signal from across the continent came through as though it were originating just a few miles away. Less than an hour later, everything was again working normally. A further check revealed that all shore stations within normal range of the *Hollyhock* were fully operational at the time and had been all through the month of November 1974. These stations were also within range of the *Dilligence*'s radios when they failed to operate during the same month. Neither coast guard ship was near any other vessels at the time their radios malfunctioned. So there was no way to tell if it was a localized atmospheric condition that affected the radio, an occurrence aboard the ships, or something else. However, neither of the vessels or their crews were any worse for their experiences.

The USCG *Hollyhock* still maintains buoys and other navigational aids, and the USCGC *Dilligence*, until recently, patroled those waters as though nothing unusual had ever happened. But there were still a few men serving about the cutter *Dilligence* who wore the "triangle" around their necks whenever the ship put out to sea.

FOURTEEN

Mona, the Isle of Mystery

Mona Island is an eerie, grotesque geological formation rising out of the depths of the sea in the passage that separates Puerto Rico from the Dominican Republic. Of all the islands in the West Indies, none looks as foreboding as Mona and its small neighbor Monita, both looming up out of the Mona Passage.

The history of Mona Island abounds with stories of bizarre, possibly supernatural occurances. Only a thin line separates legend from fact. Although many islands in the West Indies, such as Haiti, thrive on mysterious and strange goings-on, none looks more the part of the phantom isle than Mona.

The island was acquired as an American posssession when Puerto Rico became part of the United States after the Spanish-American War. It is presently under the jurisdiction of the Puerto Rican government and has become a state park. Its history records that the island has been occupied by Indians, Spanish, pirates, French, more pirates, English, more pirates, Germans, more Spanish, and Puerto Ricans. Today, modern pirates in the form of treasure hunters and drug smugglers visit Mona.

Mona Island is located where the Atlantic and the Caribbean meet. On the north side of the island, waves rolling down from the North Atlantic crash against towering cliffs that loom hundreds of feet up from the surface of the sea. The east side of the island is also lined with bluffs rising out of the ocean. Mona's south side is not quite so forbidding, for the bluffs are less precipitous and the waters near shore are shallower. Mona Island's west shore looks more like a tropical Caribbean island. A reef-protected beach extends along that side of the island, and there are several anchorages that are protected from all but the stongest westerly winds. The cave-pocked cliffs are a short distance inland. This section of Mona is as beautiful as the rest of the island is grotesque.

Goats, wild pigs, and iguana lizards up to six feet in length are found in the wooded west end of Mona. Lime, mango, and orange trees abound. The reef-protected, crystal-clear waters offer excellent diving. Dozens of species of fish inhabit the waters.

The greater part of Mona Island is one vast plateau overgrown with almost impenetrable cacti. The cacti and other vegetation camouflage numerous large holes, pits, and verticle shafts that drop anywhere from ten to a hundred feet straight down to subterranean caverns. On occasion, human remains—those of lost fishermen, treasure hunters, and victims of foul play—have been discovered in these natural death traps. Some of the bones were so old that it was impossible to determine their age.

On the plateau at the eastern end of the island stands

a coast guard lighthouse with a light range of twenty-one miles. During and right after World War II, the United States Air Force maintained a facility on Mona to observe and score practice bomb runs made on Monita, a huge coquina-like rock several miles to the north-west. The few remaining buildings, although quite deteriorated, are still used by treasure hunters and fishermen brave enough to spend a night ashore on Mona.

Sardinero and Isabel anchorages, at Mona's west end, were used by early explorers and pirates to careen* the bottoms of their ships. Mona Island probably has more natural caves per acre than any other island in the West Indies. No accurate count has been made of the caves that honeycomb the island, and some of them have never been entered by man. I visited Mona with a group of people during the month of July some years ago. One afternoon, I entered a cave whose entrance faced almost due west. After I had spent several hours probing with a metal detector for treasure there, the cavern suddenly lit up with a reddish glow so bright that we were able to turn off our lanterns. The stalactites and stalagmites looked like jagged fangs of some prehistoric monster. The cavern's beauty was frightening. There we were, over two hundred yards in from the entrance, yet there was enough light to shoot motion-picture film. There was no mystery to the phenomenon. On three days of the year, as the setting sun touches the western horizon, its rays angle directly into the cave and penetrate hundreds of feet back under Mona's plateau.

---

*Careening a vessel is to beach it at high tide. As the tide ebbs, the crew cleans and scrapes the ship's bottom.

Many names, both famous and infamous, are associated with Mona Island. Christopher Columbus is supposed to have sent a boat ashore there. It is unknown whether he accompanied the shore party. On several occasions between 1590 and 1593, ships under the command of Sir Walter Raleigh stopped at Mona. During one of those visits his men found ten to twelve dwellings; they chased the occupants into the caves and burned the houses. Several years later, Sir Francis Drake put in to Mona to repair a damaged ship and take on water.

Mona was a renowned pirate hangout. In 1699, the notorious Captain Kidd visited Mona to careen the bottom of his ship, the *Adventure Galley*. Kidd, who so ably navigated more than half the waters of the world, couldn't find his way on Mona; he became lost on the island, and it was three days before he found his way back to the camp. The list of buccaneers who stopped at Mona reads like a *Who's Who* of piracy: Blackbeard (Teach), Flood, Rackam, Avery, Bonnet, Vane, Hornigold, Bellamy, and Jennings. Even today the name of Captain Henry Jennings is synonymous with Mona Island when treasure hunters get together over a drink, for Jennings was rumored to have left one of the greatest undiscovered hoards of all time at Mona Island.

In 1715, as a fleet of Spanish treasure galleons was passing north through the Straits of Florida en route to Spain, a great hurricane bore down on the ships. After the storm passed, most of the fleet was missing. The Spaniards maintained a fleet of salvage vessels in Havana to rescue survivors and recover valuables from ships wrecked or damaged during such storms. They located a number of wrecked ships from the ill-fated 1715 fleet along the eastern coast of Florida just south of Cape Canaveral. A salvage base was established on the Cape and a salvage-and-recovery operation got under way.

Through the efforts of native divers using primitive wooden diving bells, the Spaniards recovered pieces of eight by the ton. A storage house was erected at the Cape Canaveral salvage base to hold the silver, and a continuous guard of at least sixty men at a time protected it. No less than a million silver pieces of eight were recovered during the first month of salvage.

Word of this lucrative operation soon reached Captain Henry Jennings. Being a man of great enterprise and taking into consideration the fact that England and Spain were engaged in one of their many wars, Jennings concluded that the Spanish government already had more riches than it needed. Thus, he gathered together his five-vessel fleet and headed for Cape Canaveral.

As the fleet—two ships and three sloops—moved toward its destination, unbeknownst to Jennings, England and Spain terminated hostilities. The fleet continued right into Cape Canaveral Bight and anchored. The sight of nearly three hundred pirates charging up the beach sent the Spanish guards scurrying into the cover of the nearby palmetto scrub. The pirates looted over 350,000 pieces of eight from the storehouse. Having captured their booty without the loss of a single man, the pirates jubilantly sailed away toward Jamaica. En route south, Jennings's ships fell in with a richly laden vessel en route from Porto Bello to Havana. The pirates confiscated riches including 60,000 pieces of eight, then allowed the Spanish ship to proceed, and Jennings and his men continued south to Jamaica.

A day out of Jamaica, the pirate fleet met an English

vessel whose captain informed the stunned Jennings that the war between Spain and England was over. Word of Jennings's deeds arrived in Jamaica only a few days after his ships.

With the governor's troops at their heels, Jennings and his men fled to their ships and sailed off, with most of the Spanish silver still aboard. A small amount had been spent for ammunition and supplies. A price was placed on Jennings's head for piracy.

At the time, Nassau, in the Bahamas, was a pirate stronghold. Jennings and his men headed there, but not via the direct course through the Windward Passage. Instead, they headed east and left the Caribbean through the Mona Passage. Upon reaching Mona, they anchored at Isabel anchorage. Some of the loot was divided among the pirates. Most of the silver was secreted in caves and crevices, to be reclaimed one day. It was rumored that when Jennings and his men sailed from Mona they left behind tons and tons of silver in the caves, for which they never returned.

There have been numerous attempts to recover Captain Jennings's treasure. In 1874, the Spanish government of Puerto Rico sent an expedition of salvagers to Mona to find the vast cache of silver. The mission was called off after ten days of accidents, fights, a suicide, and ghostly illusions during the nights. The searchers found no trace of treasure.

Pirates reigned over Mona intermittently for more than three centuries. It is the vestiges of piracy that have given Mona the reputation of being haunted. Periodically, there are reports of very unusual goings-on.

Down through the years, Mona has been a mecca for treasure hunters. Individuals have lived on Mona for

years in a quest to discover Jennings's silver. Just before
the United States entered World War I, the USS *Cy-clops*, doomed to vanish without a trace in a few years,
was voyaging through the Mona Passage. Her captain,
George W. Worley, ordered the ship stopped off the
west side of Mona. After several hours of examining the
island and its cliffs and caves with a telescope and binoculars, Worley ordered the *Cyclops* to get under way.
He mentioned something about treasure and his hope to
one day return to the island to seek it out.

Today, treasure hunters still visit Mona. But Jennings's silver is not all that they seek. The late F. L.
Coffman, a treaure authority and author of the 1950s,
discovered through his research a cache that had been
deposited on Mona Island in 1931. The treasure was
secreted in a cave accessible only at the very lowest tide.
The hoard, which had been destined for the United
States and supposedly consisted of thousands of cases
of Scotch whiskey, was to have been picked up by rumrunners who fell victim to some accident before reaching
the underwater cave.

The days of old and pirates bold still live during dark,
stormy nights on Mona—as many Puerto Rican fishermen will attest to. One story known by every Puerto
Rican schoolchild is that of an old pirate named Barber.
One day Barber kidnapped the daughter of a well-to-do
family, Doña Gena. He took her to Mona, where he had
a camp. She was held in a compound with a number of
other young women. One day, as Barber was setting out
from Mona, his ship was sighted by an English vessel
and a battle ensued. The English, unaware that women
were being held captive in Barber's camp, bombarded
the area. A number of shots struck the building in which
the women were being held, killing all of them. Barber

meanwhile beached his craft and fled to the plateau atop
Mona. The area where the women died is now called
Las Mujeras, or "the Women," for on dark windy nights,
they say, one can hear the wailing cries and screams of
the women who died in Barber's camp.

Another pirate, known as Portuguese, decided to retire
and spend his old age on Mona. His last days were tranquil until an obscure fisherman discovered that this man
was none other than the notorious Bartholemy Portuguese, who in his younger days had played havoc with
Spanish ships. The fisherman also learned that the government of Spain still offered a reward for the capture
of Bartholemy Portuguese—dead or alive. Being both
poor and an ex-pirate himself, the fisherman decided it
was a pity for all of that reward money to lie idle. Thus,
he plotted to kill Portuguese—for taking him alive
would be too great a risk.

The fisherman deliberately damaged his boat on a reef
off Mona so that, with the excuse of repairing it, he
could remain on the island without arousing suspicion.
Portuguese, however, was aware that many people were
after the reward, and, he was armed to the hilt. But the
fisherman was quite intent on collecting the reward and
studied Portuguese's habits and weaknesses. Although
the pirate avoided routines that might set him up for an
ambush, he made one mistake. Each morning, he went
to the same spring to fill his water bottles. One morning
as Portuguese was bent over, filling his jugs, the fisherman crept up behind him and decapitated him with one
swipe of his cutlass.

Taking Bartholemy Portuguese's head with him, the
fisherman returned to Puerto Rico to collect the reward.
However, the officials there felt that though the face

somewhat resembled Portuguese's, there was still a bit of doubt. One of the governor's assistants, a former soldier, had seen the pirate on several occasions and knew of a number of distinct scars on his body. So the fisherman set off for Mona in his boat to retrieve the rest of the pirate's body, which he had hidden in a cave called Cueva Nigra.

Arriving on Mona, the fisherman dragged his boat above the high-tide mark and made for the cave. But the headless body was nowhere to be seen. He searched Cueva Nigra and all of the nearby caves without success. Unable to collect the reward, the poor fisherman remained a poor fisherman.

Several years later he was with a group of other fisherman who were forced to spend the night on Mona because the seas were too rough to return to Puerto Rico. The men were sitting around a fire, exchanging stories. Strong winds were howling through the branches of the trees. As the night wore on, the rum flowed faster. The poor fisherman was just beginning to tell how he had nearly collected the reward for the capture of Bartholemy Portuguese when suddenly, from out of the darkness just beyond the campfire's glow, came a blood-curdling scream: *"Caigo o no caigo!"* Grabbing lanterns and torches, the fishermen went to investigate. When they reached the area in front of the Cueva Nigra cave, they froze in terror. For there, standing on a rock, was the headless form of Bartholemy Portuguese, a cutlass in one hand and in the other his severed head. Fishermen and others have reported seeing the same apparition many times since, on dark nights when gale winds howled down on the Mona Passage. Screaming women and headless pirates—fable or fact? Ask any Puerto Rican schoolboy.

One remaining mystery of Mona Island is whether any vast amount of hidden treasure reposes there today. During the last years of the nineteenth century, a German firm was engaged in mining guano (bat manure, which is processed into high-quality fertilizer) from the many accessible caves on the island. Perhaps these Germans found some of the treasure, for of all who were ever on the island, their opportunity for discovery was greatest.

In the 1930s, during the Great Depression, the federally sponsored CCC (Civilian Conservation Corps), which provided employment for young men out of work, set up a camp on Mona Island. The main function of the group on Mona was to plant trees and carve a road through the rock leading to the lighthouse. It is possible that they discovered some treasure, for young men are a curious lot.

When I visited Mona Island in 1958, my group and I spent a week exploring caves. Our search was incomplete, for one could spend a lifetime on Mona and not thoroughly search all of its caves. We did, however, locate one small cache of silver coins—hardly enough, though, to cover the cost of the expedition. We found nothing else, even though we explored numerous caves with our metal detectors.

Although the group spent several nights ashore on Mona Island, we did not hear voices of crying and screaming women, nor did we see ghosts of headless pirates. However, that does not mean that the ghostly sounds and the apparitions do not exist, for during our stay on Mona Island the nights were calm and windless. Still, when any of us wandered inland away from the shore area, there seemed to emit from each shadow, rock, and bush an aura that something was not just right. Not a feeling that we weren't alone, but more a sensation of impending doom looming over us. None of us wandered about alone. At night, we stayed aboard the vessel, a converted World War II PT boat. Others who've spent any time on Mona Island have experienced the same feeling.

Haunted, hexed or merely an imagination stirring environment, Mona Island is still a grotesquely beautful place.

FIFTEEN

Paradise Unreached

There is a little town in southeastern Pennsylvania named Conestoga, population around five thousand. The old-timers in Conestoga will tell you that their town's claim to fame is the fact that it was there, in Lancaster County, that the famous Conestoga covered wagons were developed and built during the late 1700s and early to mid-1800s. The Conestoga wagons were noted for their broad-rimmed wheels, which enabled them to go through soft sand and mud, and they figured prominently in the development of the American west.

Very few, if any, citizens of Conestoga realize that their little community also figures, even if indirectly, in one of the many continuing mysteries of the sea. For a ship was named after that little town.

The USS *Conestoga* was built in 1904 by the Maryland Steel Company at Sparrows Point, Maryland. She was used privately as a seagoing tug and salvage vessel until November 10, 1917, when the United States Navy took her over. The ship was originally assigned to the submarine force along the Atlantic coast. She also transported supplies and escorted convoys to Bermuda and the Azores. During much of her wartime career, she worked out of the Azores, escorting or towing damaged and disabled ships into safe harbors. After the war, the *Conestoga* was assigned to the Fifth Naval District at Norfolk, where she served for several years in the navy yard as a harbor tug.

The men of the "old navy" claim that there are two types of seagoing navies—the fighting navy and the working navy. The *Conestoga* belonged to the latter. Duty aboard a navy tug, however, can be rather rigorous. You are at sea in every kind of weather, working with heavy towlines solidly frozen with ice. You are continuously around dirt and grime, and while you are based near a liberty port, you are kept so busy that you rarely get ashore. Added to these afflictions is the fact that seagoing tugs are far from being the most comfortable vessels in any kind of rough sea.

In 1920, the *Conestoga* received orders to proceed to the United States Navy Base at Tutuila, Samoa, where she was to serve as a station ship. The crew was elated—for weeks to come, the main topics of discussion aboard the vessel were swaying palm trees and hula girls.

The *Conestoga* was readied for the passage and put out from Hampton Roads, Virginia, on November 18, 1920. After the ship cleared the Panama Canal, it was decided that she needed some modifications before heading out across the Pacific Ocean. Her destination was changed to San Diego, where she arrived on January 7, 1921. On February 17, she steamed up the coast for Mare Island Navy Yard. There, she underwent additional repairs and conversion.

Following a navy picture-taking session, the *Conestoga* put to sea from Mare Island on March 25. Finally, she was under way for the lands of hula dancers and swaying palm trees. There were fifty-six officers and men in the crew, but the USS *Conestoga* never reached the islands of hula girls and swaying palm trees. She vanished—no distress signals—no trace.

Then on May 17, the SS *Senator* was steaming at latitude 18 degrees, 15 minutes north and longitude 115 degrees, 42 minutes west when her lookout sighted the wreckage of a lifeboat. Closer inspection revealed a bronze letter "C" on the boat's bow. The ship's crew removed the letter, and it was sent to the Navy Department. However, no determination could be made as to whether the "C" came from one of the *Conestoga*'s boats.

During the search for the missing navy tug, one of the participating vessels, the United States submarine *R-14*, was plying an area southeast of the Hawaiian Islands. Suddenly, for a reason that no one could explain, the sub lost every source of power—both electrical and mechanical. The *R-14* lay dead in the water. Without any of its communication systems working, the crew was virtually helpless. All attempts at repairs were futile. No cause or explanation could be found. The entire crew, from skipper to mess boy, was baffled. The navy subsequently announced that one of its submarines was overdue and missing.

When everything appeared to be hopeless aboard the submarine, an obscure seaman came up with a wild idea: Sails. Thus, with her raised periscope for a mast and deck canvas cut and sewn into a square sail, she got under way. Five days later, on May 15, people aboard ships and ashore stared in disbelief as the submarine *R-14* entered the harbor at Hilo, Hawaii, under full sail. Thus ended the longest, if not the only, voyage ever made by a submarine under sail.

On June 30, 1921, the extensive search for the *Conestoga* was called off. The Navy Department declared the *Conestoga* and her crew as having been lost without a trace.

But if you ever drive through Lancaster County, Pennsylvania, stop off at Conestoga and ask any of the townsfolk what their town is famous for. They'll tell you "Covered wagons."

There is a similar story of another United States Navy seagoing tug. The United States Government Printing Office publishes a series of books called *American Naval Fighting Ships*, listing every United States Navy ship ever built, along with an explanation of its name, a brief history of its career, and an account of its final disposition. Many public libraries have these volumes so that navy veterans or anyone else can read about what happened to a given ship, even if it was decommissioned and sold to a private or foreign operator. Not only the famous ships have been chronicled; so have the most obscure vessels that ever served in the American navy.

One of the latter was the USS *Nina*, a vessel that had one of the longest active careers in the United States Navy. As the Civil War was ending, the *Nina* was launched on May 27, 1865, at Reaney & Son Shipyard in Chester, Pennsylvania. She was classified as a "fourth-rate iron screw steamer." In other words, she was one of the first navy tugboats. A month after the end of the Civil War, she was assigned to the New York Navy Yard.

In 1869, the *Nina* was transferred to the Washington Navy Yard where she was converted to a torpedo boat, a capacity in which she served until 1884. Then she was again converted, this time to a salvage tug carrying out assignments along the middle and upper Atlantic coasts.

In 1902, the *Nina* made her first extended cruise, a voyage to the Caribbean, where she served until 1905 as a tender and a supply vessel for a flotilla of torpedo boats based in that area. (The torpedo boat of that era was the forerunner of the modern destroyer.)

Based in Puerto Rico, the *Nina* also served as a lighthouse tender and a survey vessel. On December 28, 1905, she was reassigned to the Norfolk Navy Yard, where she became the navy's first submarine tender and worked with the Atlantic Fleet's infant submarine force during its pioneering operations.

At 0630 on February 6, 1910, after forty-five years of continuous service with the United States Navy, the *Nina* put to sea from Norfolk bound for Boston with a thirty-man crew. The navy's first submarine tender was last seen off the capes of the Chesapeake Bay during a moderate windstorm. That was the *Nina*'s final voyage. She was never seen nor heard from again and was stricken from the navy's records on March 15, 1910. According to *American Naval Fighting Ships*, "her loss is one of the continuing mysteries of the sea."

The USS *Nina* might be deemed just another ship that vanished at sea without a trace. Yet she had one of the longest active service records of the United States Navy;

she was the navy's first submarine tender and one of its first destroyer tenders. Unlike her namesake, Columbus's *Nina*, she went down at sea in the service of her country, rather than in the shoals as a result of neglect.

SIXTEEN

The Galloping Ghost of the Java Coast

While the *Stewart* and the other old destroyers of DES RON 29 were fighting for their lives in the South China Sea during those harrowing weeks following the Japanese attack on Pearl Harbor, other Allied ships were also taking on the Japanese in nearby waters.

The last saga of "the Galloping Ghost of the Java Coast" took place in the Sundra Strait off Java. The so-called "Galloping Ghost" had been fighting alongside the American destroyers, the Australian cruiser HMAS *Perth* and the American light cruiser *Marblehead*. The heavy cruiser *Houston* had been given the "Galloping Ghost" nickname during the opening days of the war because the Japanese had erroneously reported sinking her again and again and again.

In encounter after encounter, the Japanese engulfed all that stood in their way. Only those few outnumbered and underequipped Allied ships stood between the Japanese and a totally unopposed blitzkrieg across the eastern oceans. Knowing that their chance of victory was only slightly more than nil, the Allies fought on. They never faltered. The losses of the ships and men during the early days of the war were not, however, in vain, for their sacrifices paved the way for an eventual Allied victory. "The Galloping Ghost of the Java Coast" was one of those sacrifices.

The cruiser *Houston* is not mentioned here because of her nickname. It is due to the strange spectacle, an unexplainable and apocalypse-like episode, that she and her crew experienced during the ship's last night afloat.

On the night of February 28, 1942, the United States heavy cruiser *Houston* and the Australian heavy cruiser *Perth* were steaming through the Sundra Strait. The gallant ships were on a voyage of doom, for they were en route to engage a vastly superior Japanese naval force consisting of no less than three cruisers and ten torpedo-equipped destroyers. Both the *Houston* and the *Perth*, while steaming on ahead, were undergoing repairs to damage received in the previous day's battles.

It was the darkest of dark nights as the two ships passed through the strait. Suddenly, six strange flarelike lights appeared, bobbing in the water alongside the *Houston*. The flaming, yellowish flares resembled the round smoke pots used alongside highway construction sites. The men of the *Houston* were baffled as they stood at the rail watching the strange lights. If they were some sort of new Japanese device for illuminating enemy ships, they had never been used before. The officers and men aboard the big cruiser were justifiably concerned, for somewhere in the darkness ahead lay the enemy fleet.

The crews of the two ships felt relieved as they left the strange water lights behind. But their relief was not to last. Minutes later, another cluster of lights suddenly flared up alongside the ships. Then another. As each group of flares was left astern, another cluster would suddenly flare up alongside the ships. Even after a deliberate change in course, the floating flares continued to glow alongside the cruisers. The men aboard the two Allied ships were completely mystified by the uncanny phenomenon. And horrified, for their ships, silhouetted by the yellow glow of the flares, were perfect targets. Yet they continued on course through the Sundra Strait unmolested.

After a number of anxious moments, the ghoulish jack-o'-lanterns were left behind, as the *Houston* and *Perth* steamed on ahead into the welcome darkness.

Just before midnight, after clearing the strait, the *Houston* and *Perth* discovered the Japanese fleet lying at Banten Bay on Java's northwest coast. It would be the understatement of World War II to say that the two Allied cruisers were outnumbered and outgunned. For instead of the thirteen Japanese ships they had expected, they found themselves engaged in a battle with no less than sixty-nine enemy warships.

. The *Houston* and *Perth* steamed defiantly into the midst of the Japanese fleet with all guns blazing. Almost immediately, the *Perth* received a number of direct hits and sank within five minutes. The *Houston* fought on for another forty minutes. Receiving hit after hit, she was sustaining more punishment than her designers could ever have anticipated.

Finally, with her engines dead, her magazines flooded, and most of her guns out of action, the "Galloping Ghost of the Java Coast" began listing heavily to the starboard. As Captain Rooks was giving the order to abandon ship, a piece of shrapnel ripped through his chest, killing him instantly.

The two heroic Allied cruisers did not go down in vain. They took with them to the bottom of the Java Sea four Japanese ships. The *Houston* also damaged twelve other enemy vessels enough to put them out of action for months to come.

Survivors from the *Perth* and *Houston*, those who were not machine-gunned by the Japanese as they struggled in the water, spent the rest of the war in POW camps. It was not until their release after the war that the full story of the "Galloping Ghost of the Java Coast" was told.

After the occupation of Japan following VJ Day, Allied officers examining the enemy's weaponry files could find nothing about a device that even remotely resembled a floating yellow flare that would light up at the approach of an enemy ship. However, several of the researchers who had been historians and anthropologists during peacetime recalled that during and right after the world's most tremendous volcanic explosion in 1883, at Krakatoa on Java, there had been reports of small masses of strange floating objects in the surrounding sea, objects that gave off a dull yellow flare. Could some sort of ghostly reflection of the eruption been waiting in the water for over 50 years, to be awakened by the passing ships?

SEVENTEEN

The Devil's Jaw

Mandibula del Diablo is what the early Spanish set-tlers in California called it. Today, it is known by its English translation, The Devil's Jaw. When the early Spanish explorers stood at the top of the cliffs over-looking the formation of rocks stretching seaward, it re-minded them of a giant jaw, with each big rock giving the appearance of a huge jagged fang. The Devil's Jaw is located just north of the Santa Barbara Channel near Point Arguello, California, adjacent to the huge Vanden-berg Air Force Base complex.

The Devil's Jaw is a death trap for ships. Its menace dates back to the California gold rush days in the mid-1800s. One of the earliest recorded disasters was that of the *Edith*, which crashed onto the fangs of the Jaw in 1848. The story goes that the vessel's gold-crazed crew deliberately wrecked the *Edith* in hope of reaching the gold fields sooner.

Most of the tragedies at the Devil's Jaw have occurred on Saturdays. Bypassing most of the victims for now,

163

and jumping ahead to Saturday, September 8, 1923, we come to the most spectacular of all the disasters that have occurred in the grips of The Devil's Jaw.

On that night, the Pacific mail steamer SS *Cuba* transmitted a distress call stating that she had run aground and was sinking. She gave her position as the San Miguel Rocks just south of the Devil's Jaw. She had been carrying both passengers and cargo. Her distress calls were picked up by a squadron of fourteen United States Navy destroyers en route from San Francisco to San Diego. One of the ships, the USS *Reno*, was ordered to break formation and proceed south at flank speed to assist the stricken *Cuba*.

The other thirteen destroyers of Squadron Eleven continued on course at twenty knots toward their base in San Diego. The lead ship was the USS *Delphy*, under the command of Lieutenant Commander Donald Hunter. Commodore of the fourteen-ship fleet was Captain Edwin Watson, who flew his flag from the *Delphy*. The *Delphy*'s navigation officer was a former navigation instructor at the Naval Academy, and it was his pilotage that maintained the squadron's formation. The flotilla was steaming in three columns, with the *Delphy* at the head of the center row. They maintained a speed of twenty knots, and an average distance between vessels of 250 yards. The destroyers were returning from maneuvers off Puget Sound. They had stopped at San Francisco on their passage south and had left there that same morning. The navigation officer estimated that owing to following winds and seas, their speed over the bottom was in excess of the twenty knots that they were making through the water.

The destroyers were of World War I vintage, less than

half the size of a modern destroyer. They were of the legendary "four pipers," with their four smokestacks or funnels. The passage to San Diego was a routine voyage that should have presented no difficulties. Watson's orders were to take his ships out of San Francisco Bay, steam south for two hundred miles, pass the light at Point Argello, enter Santa Barbara Channel by turning east, and then alter the course to the southeast in order to arrive at San Diego just after daylight. However, the captain's orders made no mention of the Devil's Jaw.

Each swell, as it lifted the sterns of the ships, gave the sensation that the vessels were surfing along at a greater speed than they were actually going. In fact, the following seas were slowing the vessels down, literally creating a drag, especially in the troughs between the waves. It was a deception that would prove fatal, for the destroyers were further north than the officers on the bridge of the *Delphy* had calculated, but the officers had no way of knowing, for the California coastline was shrouded in fog, preventing the sighting of landmarks from the seaward. Shipboard radar was still years away.

During the 1920s, fixing a ship's position by radio bearings was for the most part inaccurate. The equipment was bulky and primitive, and most captains chose not to rely on it. But on occasion it did prove accurate.

At 1800 (6:00 P.M.), Captain Watson requested radio bearings from the transmitting station at Point Arguello. An earlier request had given the ship a position much farther to the north than the officers aboard the *Delphy* had calculated. Thus, the captain chose to rely on his own dead reckoning navigation. However, the 1800 radio bearings were close to his own plotted position.

The *Delphy* was the only ship that requested the radio

bearings. The other ships in the flotilla were obediently relying on their leader in the best tradition of the navy. Also, as per orders, they were maintaining radio silence, for they were on a wartime-basis drill.

As Watson and Hunter stood on the *Delphy*'s wing bridge in the chill Pacific air, they discussed how they would enter Santa Barbara Channel, between Point Honda to the north and San Miguel Island on the south. Although the channel opening was twenty miles wide, the two officers expressed concern because of the fog. It had been eight hours since they had seen any landmarks or been able to take a celestial fix. The radio fixes could not be relied on. And the fog was becoming more dense.

Shortly after 2000 (8:00 P.M.), Watson and Hunter replotted their position on the chart, comparing the dead reckoning and the radio fixes and coming up with a difference between the two. Still believing that the effect of the following seas and wind were moving them in excess of twenty knots over the bottom, the two officers became concerned that they might end up too far south and run the risk of piling up on the rocks at San Miguel as the liner *Cuba* had done a few hours earlier. "At 2100," Watson stated, "I propose to come to port to 095 degrees and enter the channel." Hunter agreed with his superior.

Shortly before 2100 (9:00 P.M.), a radioman entered the bridge with a position fix from Point Arguello, warning that the ships were still too far north to make a course change into the channel. Because of previous experiences with inaccurate radio fixes, however, Watson chose to stand by his original order and began turning the fleet at 2100. Both Watson and Hunter double-

checked their dead reckoning positions. The two officers' fixes coincided.

At exactly 2100, Watson gave the order, "Change
course to 095 degrees." As the helmsman put the wheel
over, the *Delphy* began veering to the port. The fog-
enshrouded night was shattered by two blasts of the lead
destroyer's whistle—a signal to the other ships that a
turn to the port was being made. As each ship followed
the order, it repeated the two-blast signal. The destroyer
plied on through the fog on a course just south of due
east at twenty knots.

As each ship changed direction, it caught the full force
of the wind and waves directly on its port beam. The
ships rolled heavily in the broadside waves, their masts
slashing like knives through the night air. The thickening
fog had decreased visibility to little more than a ship's
length.

The sleek hulls were cutting through the cold, black
water at nearly thirty-four feet per second. The commodore and his navigation officer were unaware that
somewhere in the sea ahead the Devil's Jaw lay waiting
for them. Each minute brought the ships 2,025 feet
closer to the fang-like rocks.

Six minutes and 12,152 feet after the turn to the east,
every man aboard the *Delphy* felt a slight bump. It was
little more than a gentle nudge. But within seconds, there
came the terrifying clanking of tearing steel scraping
against solid rock. The *Delphy* had become caught in
the fatal fangs of the Devil's Jaw. There was no escape.

Everyone on the bridge was slammed to the deck. The
wheel tore free from the grip of the helmsman's hands.
An officer instinctively leaped to his feet and thrust the
indicator lever on the engine room telegraph to "Back

Full." Below deck the bellow from broken steam lines combined with the roar of rushing water, and screaming voices drowned out the sounds of steel and rock.

The ship's white yardarm lights were switched on as her sirens screamed through the fog to warn the ships astern to change course. It was too late.

The next ship astern of the *Delphy* was the destroyer *Young*. She was steaming four hundred yards north of the *Delphy*—1200 tons of steel cutting through the water at eleven yards per second. Another four-piper, the *S. P. Lee*, was running parallel to the lead ship. From the *Lee*'s bridge it appeared that the *Delphy* was backing down. Below in the *Lee*'s engine room, the signal "Back Full," was received. Valves spun, and levers pulled. Her nine-foot propeller blades chopped into the southbound seas. She just missed the *Delphy*. The *Lee*'s officers sighed with relief at having barely missed colliding with the lead destroyer. But their relief was short-lived. It was as though the fang-like rocks leaped out of the water and grasped her hull.

An instant later, the *Young*'s hull was heaved clear out of the water as if she were ascending an incline. Then she fell back into the sea with a reverberating crash of steel against rock. The momentum of her twenty-knot speed carried her forward across the submerged pinnacles of rock, like a paper boat being dragged across a bed of nails. The USS *Young* was dying. Within ninety seconds, she was over on her side with barely a foot and a half of her hull sticking out of the water. Twenty of her crew were trapped below deck.

Next came the USS *Woodbury*, hurtling her 1200 tons shoreward at over 2,000 feet per minute. Her captain called up to the lookout to keep a sharp eye out for the

Point Arguello Light. The lookout soon called back, "The *Young* is stopped dead in the water! The *Lee* is turning hard to port! I can't see the *Delphy*, it's disappeared!"

To avoid ramming into the *Young*, the *Woodbury*'s captain shouted, "Hard right rudder!" Before she was ten degrees into the turn, the *Woodbury*'s crew felt the ship shudder for an instant and then stop. Water began pouring into her machinery spaces as her bottom peeled away. Run onto a jagged rock, she was stuck hard and fast. Her captain, knowing his ship would sink, wisely made no attempt to back off. Instead, he ordered everyone on deck and had the searchlights aimed at the rock as a warning to the other ships. The rock was later named Woodbury Rock.

The next destroyer, the USS *Nicholas*, suddenly emerged into an opening in the fog—an opening that was a confusion of glaring searchlights and flares. With her propellers thrashing full speed astern, the *Nicholas*'s momentum was still carrying her forward. Before anyone aboard could comprehend what was happening, the *Nicholas* was swept onto a cluster of submerged rocks. The captain ordered her hard astern. Amidst a purgatory of howling horns and screaming whistles, she backed free of the rocks. But her emancipation was to be short-lived. Two minutes later, the seething turbulence carried her onto another mass of rocks. She was firmly impaled on the submerged boulders. From the north, each oncoming wave swept the length of her decks, almost engulfing the entire vessel.

Into this maritime disaster steamed the USS *Farragut*. Sensing that there was something amiss ahead, the captain stopped his ship, and began to back the *Farragut* sternward toward the open sea. But looming out of the fog was the USS *Fuller*. She was unable to avoid ramming the *Farragut*. The collision caused heavy damage, and both ships were locked together. At the risk of being swept overboard by the storm-tossed seas or crushed to death between the two grinding hulls, the crews somehow managed to separate the two vessels.

The *Farragut*, although heavily damaged, miraculously manipulated her way backwards to the deeper water and escaped the trap. But the Devil's Jaw was to claim the *Fuller*. The windswept seas were forcing the ship shoreward toward another pinnacle of rocks. Her crew fought desperately to save their ship. Just as it seemed that the *Fuller* might escape, a huge wave, larger than the rest, lifted her on to the rocks, where she began to pound violently as her bottom was ripped away.

Aboard the USS *Chauncey*, the radioman handed the captain a message telling him to keep westward of the other ships. The captain assumed that there was either a man overboard or a minor collision ahead. He was unaware of the tragedy unfolding ahead behind the curtain of dense fog. All that the *Chauncey*'s crew could see ahead was a dull glow of flares and searchlights. The ship immediately backed down. Then, suddenly, her own searchlights exposed the *Young* hard on the rocks, being pounded mercilessly by crashing sea. The *Chauncey* stopped and then began to creep slowly ahead toward the *Young*, hoping to rescue the men aboard her. Then the unanticipated happened. The distance between the two destroyers began to close too fast. The surging current was spinning the *Chauncey* around. She was caught in the rip. There was a horrible sound of metal tearing against metal as the *Chauncey*'s fantail fell under the heaving *Young's* stern, where the *Young*'s hacking propellers ripped open its rescuer's stern like a can of sardines. In an instant, the USS *Chauncey*, too, became caught in the deadly grip of the Devil's Jaw.

Of the eight destroyers, only the *Farragut* was able to get away from the clench of the Devil's Jaw. Within five minutes, seven sleek United States Navy destroyers became useless hulks.

Still other ships from the squadron came plowing in, but they had been given sufficient warning that something was wrong ahead. The *Farragut*, by then out in deep water, was barely able to keep her pumps ahead of the seawater gushing into her hull. The *Marcus* and the *Sommers* were just able to steer clear of the trap awaiting them. The *Percival*, the eleventh ship in the column, struck a submerged object just as she was turning seaward. There was a grating noise as her hull scraped along the bottom. However, the huge waves that had spelled doom for seven of her sister ships saved the *Percival*. A huge swell lifted her up and away from the shoal, setting her free. Other than a few dented hull plates, she escaped unscathed.

As the fog lifted with the coming daylight, the full scope of the tragedy became visible, a graveyard of ships. There lay the *S. P Lee* (DD310) and the *Nicholas* (DD 311), both on their sides in the breakers. The *Delphy* (DD261) and the *Young* (DD 312) were on their sides, almost completely submerged. The *Chauncey* (DD 296), high and dry, was precariously wedged atop a pile of rocks. The *Woodbury* (DD309) was partially submerged, her stern in the sand and her bow high on the rocks. The *Fuller* (DD297) lay partially submerged against some rocks less than a ship's length away from the Woodbury.

In view of the magnitude of the disaster, it is miraculous that no more than twenty-three sailors perished. The fact that more lives were not lost can be attributed to good seamanship, well disciplined crews, and numerous acts of heroism. Chief Boatswain's Mate Arthur Peterson was one of the heroes that night.

Chief Peterson was serving aboard the *Young*, which was perched precariously on the rocks. Groping his way through the darkness, the chief reached a point on the capsized hull directly over the boatswain's locker. Taking a deep breath, Peterson submerged himself in the dark, cold water and swam until he found a hatch leading into the locker. He groped around the black interior until his lungs were ready to rip open. Just as he was about to give up and return to the surface, he found what he was looking for—a coil of manila line.

Upon reaching the surface, Peterson climbed back aboard the overturned hull of the *Young*. After several minutes' rest, he secured one end of the line to the ship and the other end around his waist. Then he reentered the dark surging water and began swimming toward the *Chauncey*, which was wedged tightly between two rocks. Although the distance between the two ships was less than fifty yards, the wind and the currents, plus the weight of the line he was carrying, gave the chief the feeling that he was swimming for miles. With each stroke, his arms became heavier, and he wondered if he would be able to lift each one for the next stroke. He was swallowing as much seawater as air. Because of the burning sensation of salt water on his eyes, he closed them and swam on blindly. Finally, when he felt that he couldn't make another stroke, he felt anxious hands from the *Chauncey* reaching down to pull him from the water. Over the roar of the wind and water, Peterson heard a cheer break out from his shipmates still aboard the *Young*.

Removing the line from around his waist, he secured it to the *Chauncey*. Then he called over to his shipmates to pull themselves along the line to the safety of the *Chauncey*. The oil-smeared survivors from the *Young* all made it to safety.

But Chief Peterson was not finished. He secured one end of another line to the rail of the *Chauncey* and the other end around his waist. Then he swam ashore, where he secured the line to a boulder. Other sailors followed suit and eventually established a network of lines from ship to ship and ship to shore. The action of Peterson and others that Saturday night, without any doubt, kept the number of lives lost to a minimum. How many other acts of heroism that night went unheralded will never be known.

Within a week of the tragedy, the navy began an inquiry into the largest peacetime disaster in its history—a disaster that cost over $13,000,000 in wrecked ships and twenty-three lives within a period of five minutes. The court hearing was held in San Diego. Secretary of the Navy Denby insisted that the hearings be made public so that the responsible officers would be known to the press.

Captain Watson's defense was that the radio bearings were inaccurate. However, this defense was shattered when it was revealed that the *Delphy* had received, only minutes before the disaster, a warning message from

Point Arguello that the squadron was too far north of the Santa Barbara Channel.

After two and a half weeks of testimony, the court of inquiry handed down the decision that the tragedy was the result of poor seamanship on the part of Watson.

On October 24, 1923, Watson and his subordinate officers were brought to trial. The defendants included the captains of the seven wrecked destroyers, on the grounds that the navy never advocated the blind following of any leadership. Lieutenant Commander Hunter and Watson's navigation officer were also ordered to stand trial.

As a result of the court-martial, Captain Watson lost 150 numbers, which meant that he would be passed over for future promotion by 150 officers junior to him. In other words, he would never again receive a promotion during his naval career. He was assigned to permanent shore duty.

Lieutenant Commander Donald Hunter lost 100 numbers on the promotion list, and along with the six other destroyer captains, he forever lost the right to command.

The public clamored that the navy had been too soft on the men responsible for the loss of its seven latest destroyers. Even so, some of the officers were eventually vindicated, and among them there emerged during World War II a commodore, two battleship captains and two admirals.

Probably the briefest summary of the disaster at Devil's Jaw was the one written in the logbook at Arguello Light: "Saturday, September 8, 1923, at Point Pedernales or Point Honda on Pacific Coast north of Arguello on Saturday night, seven United States destroyers were wrecked by running on the rocks at intervals of two minutes. High seas and heavy fog." That neatly sums up the greatest peacetime naval disaster in the history of the United States.

For years afterwards, sightseers could stand on the cliff overlooking the Devil's Jaw and look down at the rusting hulks of the dead ships as the currents swirled around them and the waves broke over what was left of their superstructures. Scrap collectors stripped whatever they could from the ships at low tide.

Even today, the relentless sea continues to work away at what little is left of the seven once-sleek destroyers—a half submerged boiler, some scattered hull sections, frames that are more rust than steel, and a few jagged steel plates that once were part of the USS *Chauncey*'s hull.

But the fang-like rocks of the Devil's Jaw have remained unchanged—as they await their next victims.

Some questions still remain. Although it was specifically claimed that most of the ships wrecked at the Devil's Jaw were the result of human error or weather, certain aspects are still not clear. For instance, why did the radio bearings from Point Arguello, which had been so notoriously unreliable, suddenly become accurate just five minutes before the destroyer tragedy? What made Captain Watson keep his ships going at a speed of twenty knots while steaming eastward through thick fog instead of reducing speed, which would have been a normal reaction, especially with visibility reduced to just a little more than a ship's length? Would a radio warning from the *Delphy* immediately after she grounded have saved any of the other ships? Why did the six other destroyer captains blindly follow the *Delphy* to its doom when there were no navy regulations requiring that they do so? Why have so many other tragedies at the Devil's Jaw occurred on Saturdays?

The *Yankee Blade* was loaded with $153,000 in pure gold shipped by the Paige-Bacon Company of San Francisco during California's Gold Rush. She was feeling her way south through thick fog when contrary currents swept into Mandibula del Diablo. Some of the victims were miners trying to swim ashore from the disintegrating ship with bags of gold dust stuffed in their pockets.

On Saturday, July 8, 1911, the steamer *Santa Rosa* was heading for San Francisco when she was swept onto the rocks and stranded in the clutches of the Devil's Jaw. Fortunately, there were no casualties in this wreck.

Other vessels that fell victim to the Devil's Jaw on a Saturday include the *Robert Sutton*, the *Golden Horn*, the SS *Harvard*, the *Sea Boy*, and a yacht, the *Suomi*, aboard which five people died in 1955, when she, too, was caught on the same rocks.

However, not all victims of the Devil's Jaw have been ships and yachts. On Saturday, May 11, 1907, a great number of lives were lost when a Southern Pacific special passenger train was roaring through the night from Los Angeles to San Francisco. The train's speed was over fifty-five miles an hour as she raced along the section of tracks that ran atop the bluffs overlooking the Devil's Jaw. The train was making a special run with Shriners from Buffalo, New York, and Reading, Pennsylvania, who had just finished a conclave in Los Angeles and were on a sight-seeing trip to San Francisco. The engineer heard a sharp crack, and an instant later the train was off the rails and plowing a hundred yards along a ditch. When the train finally came to a stop, the dining car had telescoped into the baggage car. Thirty-six people died. Investigators were never able to provide an accurate determination as to what had caused the wreck. To this day, the official records read "Cause unknown."

With so many mysterious disasters connected to the Devil's Jaw, is it possible that something beyond human or atmospheric causes could be responsible for the various tragedies along that eerie stretch of California coast?

EIGHTEEN

The Ghost and the Lighthouse

In 1851, the Great Exposition of London was held in Hyde Park. The event was the nineteenth century's version of the world's fair and other expos of modern times. The major building at the Great Exposition was an iron structure that reached 152 feet straight up into the air. Fairgoers from all over England came to see and climb the great tower. The structure remained for several years after the other exhibits had been removed. Then, one day, workmen began to carefully dismantle the lofty edifice. Piece by piece, the daring iron workers unrigged the tower. As each section was removed, it was code marked so that it might be reassembled elsewhere with a minimum of difficulty. Shortly after the disassembly was completed, the pieces, which had become a huge iron jigsaw puzzle, were loaded onto wagons and delivered to several Thames River wharfs. Next, they were loaded into the holds of three ships that were towed down the river to the sea. Soon they were en route across the Atlantic.

Great Issacs Rock is located on the western fringes of the Bahamas some twenty miles north of Bimini and fifty-five miles east of Fort Lauderdale. At its longest point, it measures but three-quarters of a mile. The surrounding waters abound with jagged coral reefs. It was to this rock that the three ships with the disassembled sections of the Hyde Park obelisk came in 1859. Most of the same workers who had taken apart the tower were aboard the ships. They would reassemble it on the lonely rock.

While the construction was going on, a spectral phenomenon occurred that made most of the workmen want to abandon the project and leave the island rock. They had seen the ghost of the "Gray Lady."

Many years earlier, during a gale, a British square-rigger was ripped to pieces on the rocks just off the rock. There was but one survivor—a tiny infant. The child had been placed in a barrel that washed onto Great Issacs Rock. Salvagers found the baby several days later. The child, none the worse for its experience, was taken to Bimini Island and eventually returned to relatives in England. According to local inhabitants, this was only the beginning of the story. Just before each full moon, the ghost of the baby's mother, who perished in the wreck, would walk the length of the island weeping for her child.

It was this ghost that so badly spooked the workmen. But with the ships gone, a persuasive construction captain managed to get the structure re-erected. Upon completion, a powerful light was mounted atop the fifteen-story tower, and red and white stripes were painted around the new lighthouse—a giant barber pole rising out of the sea. It was named Victoria Light in honor of the empire's queen. Today, it is known as Great Issacs Light. The workmen sailed back to England. The lighthouse keepers took over, and mariners had a new light to navigate by.

But "The Gray Lady of Great Issacs Light," as the haunting spirit was known, continued her regular visits several nights before each full moon. A number of men signed on as lighthouse keepers only to resign from their posts after one month—the ghostly visits compelled them to leave. The phantom haunting went on until after the turn of the century. Finally, one night, a zealous head lightkeeper, who was also a layman of the church, performed a religious ritual along the Gray Lady's path that convinced her that the child was safe. She never returned—or so goes the story. But there are those who swear that on dark and stormy nights between three-quarters and a full moon, the wailing voice of a crying woman can be heard coming from the rocks around Great Issacs Light.

Down through the years, the towering structure that was the pride of the 1851 Great Exposition of London was unheralded by the world except for passing sailors and the men who kept the light burning. That is until August 4, 1969, when two of the lighthouse's keepers, Ivan Major and B. Millings simply vanished, never to be seen again.

A Miami fisherman, Bruce Mounier, claims that shortly after the disappearance, he was in his boat a short distance from Great Issacs Light when he saw what he believed to be two underwater UFOs—"large gray egg-shaped objects, each about sixty feet long moving through the water at a high rate of speed just below the surface. I couldn't believe what I was seeing, but I saw them. I saw what I saw!"

If you were ever in Fort Lauderdale during the early 1970s and stopped by one of the larger marinas, chances are that you might have seen a giant of a man, six feet, three inches of walking muscle. He could have stepped from the pages of "Terry and the Pirates," a leading comic strip of that era. The tattoos enwrapping his arms told of his many years in the navy. His tan cap and uniform and his boating shoes marked him as a charter boat captain. His name was John Carpenter.

When rower John Fairfax completed his transatlantic row in 1969, John Carpenter greeted him on his arrival in Florida. However, when Fairfax told of his encounter with two UFOs, Carpenter scoffed at the story as a publicity hoax. For well over a year, Carpenter referred to Fairfax's story as a "wild tale of the sea." Now, thirty years later, Carpenter has long since stopped scoffing at stories of UFOs.

One summer night in 1970, the red-bearded seafarer was aboard his charter yacht cruising in the waters just off Great Issacs Light. The passengers and mate were asleep below. The moon was full and the sea flat calm. Carpenter was looking ahead, planning to turn west and cross the Gulf Stream to Florida. It was shortly after midnight. He had a sudden feeling that something was different, strange, but he couldn't tell what. Then he discovered what was wrong. The foredeck, which should have been reflecting the white light of the full moon, was casting a greenish reflection.

"I leaned out the cabin window and looked up. I couldn't believe what I was seeing. Directly above the boat were two glowing, greenish disk-shaped objects. They were just hovering there. I was totally awestruck. I watched the two objects for . . . I don't know how long. I was about to call the others to come up and see, when the two objects plunged into the sea with hardly a splash. I watched their greenish glows disappear far down into the depths." John Carpenter, who no longer scoffs at UFO reports, went on, "I didn't report the incident when I reached Fort Lauderdale because people tend to ridicule you when you tell them that you witnessed something that might be supernatural."

Well before the term *UFO* became part of the English language, there were similar reports of fiery flying objects.

It was daylight, but the sun had not yet lifted above the horizon. The weather was clear and balmy as the motor vessel *Atlantic City* plied westward less than a day away from her destination in Newport News, Virginia. A long Atlantic swell running from the east periodically gave the freighter's stern a gentle heave upward. It was an ordinary summer morning in 1955. Most of the crew were still sleeping; the ship was on autopilot.

W. J. Morris of Llantrissan, South Wales, was on lookout duty atop the *Atlantic City*'s bridge. Soon, it would be time to awaken the rest of the crew and ready the ship for entering port. Morris was joined by the officer of the watch, who chatted for a few minutes before returning below to the wheelhouse.

Suddenly, the officer gave out a yell. The ship was running wild—zigzagging and circling erratically. The two men saw what Morris later described as a great ball of fire traveling rapidly and heading directly for the ship. It was on a collision course with the *Atlantic City*.

Panicking, Morris began to jump over the wind dodger to the foredeck below. The mate grabbed him and pulled him back to the bridge. The two terrified men lay there, covering their faces. Hearing no noise whatsoever, just absolute silence, they looked up. The fireball was nearly upon them. Its glare was intense. Making no roar or sound at all, it passed directly over the ship, clearing the mastheads by what seemed to be only inches. The men leaped to their feet. But the phenomenal ball of fire was gone. The only evidence that it had existed, besides two frightened seamen, was a strange turbulence on the surface of the water where it had plunged into the sea.

The two men raced to the wheelhouse to regain control of the veering ship. It took several minutes to steady the ship. The *Atlantic City*'s gyro compass was dead, and all the electrical gear, failing to function during the rest of the voyage, had to be overhauled upon reaching port.

If Dr. Allen Hynek, the world's leading UFOlogist at the time, or some other eminent astronomer had been aboard the *Atlantic City* and witnessed the phenomenon, could he have identified it? If so, what was it?—a meteorite, a piece of space junk reentering our atmosphere, an illusion, or a UFO?

NINETEEN

Titanic: A Truth Stranger Than the Truth

Whenever the tragic story of the *Titanic* seems about to become passé, the subject reemerges with new undersea discoveries or a different movie version. Undoubtedly, more books, movies, and TV specials have been produced about the *Titanic* than any other steamship in history.

Just before midnight on April 14, 1912, the huge "unsinkable" White Star liner was plying her way westward on her maiden voyage through the North Atlantic. The only disturbance on the dark surface of the mirror flat sea was the big liner's wake. The 1,316 passengers were in a gay, festive mood. The night was clear. A frigid chill permeating the air was all that kept the night from being perfect—for the RMS *Titanic* was near the southern flow of icebergs that drifted down from the Arctic. The rest is history.

The "unsinkable" *Titanic* struck one of the icebergs, and within a few hours, before any other ships could reach the scene, plunged to the bottom of the frigid waters of the North Atlantic. Of the 2,201 passengers and crew aboard, only 711 were saved. Reports on the sinking abounded with stories of both heroism and cowardice. Of the many accounts that have been written about that night, probably the best known is Walter Lord's book *A Night to Remember*, which was made into a motion picture. And as 1997 came to a close, a new spectacular blockbuster film called—what else—*Titanic* was produced at a price of $200 million dollars. That is considerably more than the original ship itself cost. The three-hour epic, written and directed by James Cameron, basically uses the disaster as a background for the main story line, a love affair. But these have one thing in common other than the ship itself—they all have been written after the fact.

Of all the authors of books and stories about ships and the sea down through the years, only a small minority, such as Jack London, Richard Dana, Joseph Conrad, Herman Melville and Hammond Innes, were men who really knew the sea, for they had been sailors or mariners themselves.

Another was Morgan Robertson, a merchant seaman, who wrote a book about an "unsinkable" passenger liner, which, while carrying the elite of two continents on its maiden voyage, struck an iceberg and sunk. Instead of naming the ship in his story the *Titanic*, Robertson called it the *Titan*, and his book was called *The Wreck of the Titan*. Although his book was written as fiction, nearly all of the events in it parallel the actual story of the *Titanic*.

Both ships were built to be unsinkable. Both the true and fictional versions had incidents of heroism and cowardice. Both the *Titanic* and the *Titan* were on their maiden voyages. Both sank after striking an iceberg. The elite of society from both sides of the Atlantic made up their passenger lists. Each sinking occurred during the month of April. Only one-third of those aboard each ship survived. The *Titanic* and the *Titan* both carried insufficient lifeboats. And the officers of the *Titan*, like those of the *Titanic*, had been pressed by the ship's owner to establish a new North Atlantic speed record.

The *Titanic* and the *Titan* both had three propellers. And just before each ship plunged to the bottom, their boilers could be heard tearing loose from their foundations.

Except for a condensed version in *McClure's* magazine, *The Wreck of the Titan* was rejected by one publisher after another. Morgan Robertson, sailor-author, died without seeing his version of the sinking of the "unsinkable" ship published in book form. In their rejection slips, the publishers all offered the same reason why the manuscript of *The Wreck of the Titan* was being turned down. They explained that the editors felt that the story was beyond all believability and that the events depicted couldn't possibly happen to an "unsinkable" ship. For, you see, Morgan Robertson wrote his book in 1898, fourteen years before the R.M.S. *Titanic* struck an iceberg and slid beneath the waves into history.

TWENTY

Another Ghost Ship

Allied convoymen of World War II considered the magnetic north, or the Arctic seas, the grimmest, the harshest, the cruelest run of all. The frozen north has been explored and reexplored many times over, and it remains an area of desolation, mystery, and death. The polar seas have always been associated with the more occult sagas of the oceans. But they do, at times, yield up one of their many secrets and give an answer to some mystery of many years earlier. At other times, they release only a clue—just enough to make the original mystery even more peculiar.

One of the most puzzling enigmas of the frozen north concerns the famed "ghost of the Arctic sea." The SS *Baychimo* was a 1,300-ton steel, twin-screw ship. The steamer, owned by the Hudson Bay Company, joined their sealing fleet in 1921. Her predecessor, the schooner *Lady Kindersly*, had been crushed by polar pack ice the year before.

The *Baychimo* was based at Vancouver, British Columbia. For nine consecutive years, she worked the Beaufort Sea on Alaska's north coast and the treacherous McClintock Channel deep in the Arctic archipelago. No other vessel had been able to work those waters for more than two seasons. The *Baychimo* had established a record. And she would soon establish another record—a much more bizarre one.

During a raging blizzard that roared down out of the Arctic on October 1, 1931, the *Baychimo* became trapped in a field of pack ice in the Chukchi Sea off the northwest coast of Alaska. More than a million dollars worth of seal skins were crammed in her holds. Captain Cornwall and his sixteen-man crew stayed aboard the vessel for nearly a month after it became icebound. However, when grinding ice appeared to be straining the ship's hull plates, the men set up camp on a nearby beach area within eyesight of the vessel. Cornwall believed that if his ship survived the grinding pack ice, she would float free with the spring thaw.

Just a month after the *Baychimo* became trapped in the ice, another storm bore down on the vessel. But this time it came out of the south, bringing a warm front with it. The blow lasted nearly a week. When it passed, the *Baychimo* was nowhere in sight. The crew discovered that her ice anchors had torn loose and the *Baychimo* had floated away. After a brief search, the crew packed up and trudged fifty miles back to Point Barrow.

Eskimos reported sighting the *Baychimo* about forty-five miles southwest of where she had broken loose. An expedition set out in pursuit of the drifting ship, but when the men reached the area, all they found was open water.

Five months later, in the summer of 1932, the *Bay-*

chimo was sighted near Herschel Island, over one thousand miles to the east of her last reported position. This time a group of gold hunters discovered her. The prospectors boarded the ship and found her in excellent condition. However, lacking the ability to fire up her boilers and get her under way, they abandoned her.

In 1933, near Point Barrow, a thousand miles back to the west, the *Baychimo* was once again sighted. This time thirty Eskimo hunters found her. They boarded her from their small boats and kayaks and began carrying off everything they could. However, before they could finish looting the *Baychimo*, a snowstorm engulfed the vessel. For ten days, the Eskimos were marooned aboard the wayward ship. Their boats were swept away before they had a chance to haul them aboard. Finally, when the *Baychimo* drifted into some pack ice, the Eskimos fled the ship and worked their way ashore, losing seven of their number in the process.

In 1934, the *Baychimo* was sighted by the schooner *Trader*. A boarding party set out for the derelict vessel. When they climbed aboard, they found broken bales of furs littering her decks, mineral ore samples scattered about the cabins, books and charts strewn about the bridge, and everything, in general, in a state of disarray as a result of the Eskimos' looting. The ship itself, however, was still in a seaworthy condition, but the members of the boarding party were unable to fire up the boilers and engines, and their own ship was too small to tow the *Baychimo*.

Down through the years and through World War II, various sightings of the *Baychimo* were reported by whaling ships, Eskimos, prospectors, and exploration parties. A National Geographic Society bulletin described the *Baychimo* thus: "She always evades capture."

The last reported sighting was by Eskimos in March 1956. The ship was trapped in pack ice and drifting northward in the Beaufort Sea. Where she is today, no one knows. Having survived over a quarter of a century of aimless drifting in the polar seas, she may have eventually frozen solidly in a huge mass of ice. Or maybe the *Baychimo* is still drifting aimlessly somewhere far up in the magnetic north.

TWENTY-ONE

Revenge of the Sea

Half a world away from where the seal hunting ship *Baychimo* had been playing cat and mouse with searchers for twenty-five years, another seal hunt was taking place. The 1952 seal-hunting season had begun at 7:00 A.M. on March 23. The hunters from five Norwegian sealing ships, the *Buskoy*, *Pels*, *Ringsel*, *Brattind*, and *Varglint*, were wading amongst the newborn pups and swinging their clubs so wantonly and effectively that they had to gauge each step carefully to keep from stumbling over the dead babies. The adult seals lay in the water, helplessly watching their offspring being slaughtered. They were unaware that they themselves would soon fall victim to the seal hunters' rifles.

Years of slaughter have practically obliterated the fur seal population. With other breeds practically eliminated, the harp and hooded seals have become the prey of choice for the modern seal hunter. The adult seal's fur is hard, almost bristly. But for the first four days of the pup seal's life, its fur is soft and smooth—just the way women like it for their coats. The adult seals are slaughtered for their blubber and hides.

The heroic seal hunters from the five ships annihilated herd after herd of helpless seals with bravado.

During the winter months, when their ships cannot penetrate the Arctic ice to reach the sealing grounds, the sealers' prime victim is the bottle nose dolphin. Although the sealers refer to them as whales, they are actually porpoises—the friendliest creatures in the sea.

There has been much speculation as to what kind of a man it takes to kill a helpless baby seal. Many do it because it is the only livelihood they know, inherited from generations of forebears. Some do it simply for the sake of killing. Others do it out of some form of perverted satisfaction they derive from slaughtering helpless creatures. Whatever the reason, baby seals go on dying.

But when man tampers with nature, sooner or later nature will go on a rampage and settle the score. And that is the fate that befell the *Buskoy*, *Pels*, *Ringsel*, *Brattind*, and *Varglint* during the 1952 seal-hunting season.

The crews of the five ships, having slaughtered and skinned thousands of baby seals, loaded them aboard their ships, began concentrating on the adult cows and bulls alike. It took only a short while for the white ice flows to become red with blood from the slaughter.

Then the five ships received a radio warning that a gale was bearing down on them from the east. Their greed prevailing, the hunters continued with the slaughter. They went on killing until it was too late—for once the wrath of nature bore down on them and their ships, it became impossible for them to escape. Windswept ice floes closed in, preventing any escape. It was the hunters who were now helpless.

Nothing was ever heard again from the seal-killing ships. The *Buskoy*, *Pels*, *Ringsel*, *Brattind*, *Varglint*, their crews and the seventy-seven hunters were swept into oblivion. Nature had brought a just end to those who were attempting to upset her balance.

TWENTY-TWO

Ghosts at Sea

For many years, at the Cities Service Oil Company's corporate headquarters in New York City there hung a photograph of two seamen who died aboard one of the company's tankers and were buried at sea. "What's unusual about a picture of two deceased company employees?" one might ask. Many maritime writers consider this incident to be one of the most baffling mysteries of the sea. On December 2, 1929, the Cities Service gasoline tanker *Watertown* was steaming south from San Pedro, California, toward the Panama Canal. While the tanker was off the coast of Mexico, tragedy struck aboard the vessel. Two deckhands working near the cargo tank area died of asphyxiation caused by gasoline fumes.

Two days later, on December 4, the ship's captain, Keith Tracy, read the sermon for burial at sea just before sunset. Minutes later, the bodies of James T. Courtney and Michael Meehan were committed to the deep in

1,400 feet of water. The SS *Watertown* continued her voyage south.

The two deceased sailors had been very popular with their shipmates, and depression enveloped the crew. However, the next day the feeling of grief was suddenly replaced first by disbelief, and then terror.

Just twenty-four hours after Courtney and Meehan were buried at sea, the ship's first mate who was standing on the *Watertown*'s wing bridge, called the captain's attention to what appeared to be two men swimming out in the open sea. Soon Captain Tracy and the crew were lining the rail. The vessel slowed down within forty feet of the swimmers. "It's Courtney and Meehan," screamed Monroe Atkins, the ship's chief engineer. The men aboard the *Watertown* recognized the swimmers as their dead shipmates. As the tanker eased alongside the two men in the water, they vanished.

"We were doing about ten knots," recalled Captain Tracy later, "and they kept reappearing and keeping up with us."

Every man aboard the *Watertown* agreed that the two apparitions were, without doubt, their two deceased shipmates. As the ship changed direction, so did the swimmers—keeping parallel with the vessel. Examination with binoculars verified that the two swimmers were definitely Courtney and Meehan. The apparitions remained with the ship for several days, until the *Watertown* was just off Balboa and ready to enter the Panama Canal.

After the *Watertown* entered the Canal Zone, the two swimmers were seen no more. The ship exited the canal and entered the Gulf of Mexico, and the passage north to New Orleans passed without incident.

Captain Tracy and Chief Engineer Atkins submitted a complete report on the fatal accident and reappearance. Company officials, skeptical at first, conceded that something strange was going on after the entire crew verified the happenings. Captain Tracy was furnished with a camera and film for the return voyage to California.

The *Watertown* steamed back south through the Gulf of Mexico to Colón where she again entered the Panama Canal. That segment of the passage was without incident. However, the tanker had no sooner exited the canal and entered the Pacific Ocean when the two swimmers appeared again. It was always the same. They swam parallel to the *Watertown* on whatever course the tanker was headed.

As soon as there was sufficient light, Captain Tracy readied the camera. It was a box camera and held an eight-exposure roll of film. The captain exposed the entire roll on the two swimming apparitions. The camera, with the film still in it, was then placed in the ship's safe. After the pictures were taken, the two swimming ghosts were never seen again.

When the *Watertown* reached port and docked, the camera, with the film, was removed from the safe in the presence of Cities Service officials. It was then taken to a photographic laboratory, where the film was developed. The captain and the company officials gathered around the darkroom man as he held the still wet roll of film up to the light. Straining their eyes, they huddled in as close as the room allowed. The first exposure was blank. The second and third frames were, due to camera movement, blurred beyond recognition. The next four pictures were blurred and showed only water.

The eighth and last frame brought a feeling of relief to the captain and chief engineer. The others were astounded. The last picture showed two slightly blurred human images swimming alongside the ship. The negative was printed, and the resulting picture clearly showed two faces resembling the ghostly swimmers of the *Watertown*'s crew—James T. Courtney and Michael Meehan swimming alongside the ship.

After seeing the print, the rest of the crew all agreed that one face was definitely that of Meehan, and that the other resembled Courtney. Friends and relatives of the two dead sailors positively identified the faces as belonging to the deceased.

For many years an enlargement of the photograph of Courtney and Meehan in the water alongside the *Watertown* hung in Cities Service's New York office. Now, almost three-quarters of a century later, there still is no earthly explanation for the swimming ghosts.

TWENTY-THREE

The Sinking Ships of the Rising Sun

Japanese who earn their living from the sea accept its mysteries as a way of life. Their folklore is permeated with stories of sea monsters, demons, ghost ships, and other mysteries. A bit of research into Japanese maritime history quickly provides more than enough cases to justify such apprehension. Many of these mysteries are quite distinct from incidents of ships disappearing without a trace in other parts of the world.

On September 11, 1952, when the fishing vessel *Myolin Maru II* returned to port, her entire crew swore they had witnessed an island rising up out of the sea 320 miles south of Tokyo. Their statements drew considerable attention. Within a few days, three research vessels, the *Shikene*, the *Shimyo Maru* and the *Kaiyo Maru 5*, were en route to the site of the strange new island.

On September 23, the scientists aboard the *Shimyo Maru* made dramatic instrument recordings of a submarine volcano exploding northeast of the Bonin Islands. On the sea's surface, they observed a yellow vapor rising from the ocean near two projections of newly exposed rock that rose out of the water. The sea around them was the color of mustard. The newly discovered volcano was named Myojin-shoo. Exploring the area with the *Shimyo Maru* was the *Shikene*. The third ship, the *Kaiyo Maru 5*, a fishery research vessel, was still en route to the area. She had not yet established radio contact with the first two ships. When the *Kaiyo Maru 5* didn't arrive on the twenty-fourth, the other two ships, thinking she had turned around, returned to port.

When they arrived back in Tokyo, they learned that the *Kaiyo Maru 5* had sailed from there on September 21 and had not been seen nor heard from since. Scores of ships and aircraft set out to search for the missing research vessel.

After days of searching, vestiges of wreckage coated with a strange yellow substance were found and identified as pieces of the missing vessel. The flotsam was taken back to Tokyo, where laboratory tests disclosed that the strange coating on the shattered planks was made of pumice flakes (lava flakes or powder). Further study showed these to be identical to scrapings taken from rock specimens collected from the volcano Myojin-shoo. The fact-finding board set up by the government of Japan tentatively concluded that the *Kaiyo Maru 5* had been totally destroyed by an underwater explosion as she sat directly over the submarine volcano Myojin-shoo. Aside from the few planks, no other trace of the ship or those aboard were found.

Three years later, another research ship, the *Shihyo Maru*, was taking soundings along the volcanic Myojin Reef, near where the *Kaiyo Maru 5* had disappeared. Then, some unexplained fate overwhelmed her—for the

Shihyo Maru, too, was never heard from again. Even though an extensive search was carried out, no trace of the vessel was ever found. In fact, an investigation disclosed that during the three years between the times when the two research vessels vanished, no less than nine other ships had mysteriously disappeared in the same general location.

That area of the Pacific Ocean is vast and subject to sudden storms; it is the Eastern Hemisphere's equivalent to the Devil's or Bermuda Triangle. In fact, Japanese and other seamen from that part of the world often refer to it as the "Devil's Sea."

During the nineteenth century, scores of tea-carrying clipper ships vanished in those waters, the most renowned being the *Caliph* sailing from Foochow, China, to New York with a cargo of tea. Ironically she had been built to challenge the speed records of the *Cutty Sark* and the *Thermopylae*.

On November 23, 1921, a large wooden schooner, with a 223-foot-long hull of clipper ship proportions, sailed from Kishiro, Japan, with a cargo of coal bound for Tshihma. The vessel, the *Bansei Maru 10*, was never seen again. A few months later, on February 14, 1922, another large schooner, the *Kibi Maru I*, also loaded with coal, sailed from Muroran for Yokohama. She, too, was never heard from again. Both voyages were coastal passages.

In November 1923, the Japanese government-owned railroad ferry *Iki Maru* disappeared off the southeast coast of Japan. Exactly one year later, the antiquated, forty-four year old steamship *Kagawa Maru* put to sea from Muroran with a cargo of coal destined for Kamaishi. She, too, became a victim of the "Devil's Sea."

The American cargo ship *Elkton*, owned by the Lykes Brothers Steamship Co. departed Shanghai on December 30, 1926, for New York. The last known position radioed from her before she vanished was 14 degrees north latitude and 136 degrees east longitude in the "Devil's Sea."

For some reason coal-carrying ships seem to rate high on the list of ships vanishing in those waters. On March 10, 1928, it was the *Kashin Maru*, laden with coal. On February 19, 1934, it was the *Banyei Maru*, also carrying coal. And on and on. The victims have ranged from large military ships to tiny sampans from obscure fishing villages. And the disappearance of ships is not the only mystery.

"The Galloping Ghost of Nansei Shoto" was the name aptly applied to a strange radar phenomenon witnessed by American sailors during World War II. The "ghost" was particularly prevalent in the area of Okinawa. During the pre-invasion strikes against that island early in 1945, radarmen on United States warships would periodically pick up a large, slowly moving object less than one hundred miles southeast of the island. Combat air patrols from the carrier force would be dispatched to the area. As the planes neared the "target," the radar image would become fuzzy; and before the planes were within visual distance, the image would vanish altogether. This was a frequent occurrence, and it always took place near the same coordinates. The only thing known about the phenomenon was that neither the Allies nor the Japanese had any device that might have created the radar apparition.

It has been well over fifty years since radarmen on warring United States Navy ships sailed the waters off

Okinawa. Still, today, an occasional ship or aircraft will report having picked up on its radar the image of "the Galloping Ghost of Nansei Shoto."

For the reader who may surmise that events in the "Devil's Sea" are just part of normal maritime mishaps and are not unusual for any of the world's oceans, the Japanese Maritime Safety Agency released the following in 1973:

    1968 . . . 521 fishing vessels went missing.
    1970 . . . 435 fishing vessels went missing.
    1972 . . . 471 fishing vessels went missing.

The list includes only fishing vessels—no yachts, no warships, no freighters, no liners, and no research ships, all of which have also gone missing in this area. Who knows what the statistics for those are?

TWENTY-FOUR

The Greatest Sailor of Them All

There is the America's Cup Race. And there is the Whitbread Round the World Race. And there are several single-handed around the world races such as Around Alone 1998–1999, the Vendee Globe Challenge and the BOC Challenge, plus single-handed transatlantic races. To participate in the America's Cup, one has to be an excellent sailor. To participate in the Whitbread, one must be even better. And to sail alone in the single-handed races around the world, one has to be the best of sailors, the finest seaman, a no-mistake navigator, a ship repairer, a sailmaker, a captain, a medic, a cook, a cabin boy—and maybe a little peculiar. As Jim Flannery, a writer for *Soundings Magazine*, wrote when quoting Whitbread Race participant Ross Field, such races are "75 percent boredom and 25 percent terror."

But what does it take to sail alone around the world with no radio, no radar, no electronic navigation devices, no self-steering, and instead of a chronometer—an alarm clock with the minute hand missing? And, of course, no international rescue agency or anyone monitoring your location or well-being.

It was more than a hundred years ago that Joshua Slocum, a retired American sea captain, completed the first solo circumnavigation ever in a thirty-six-foot yawl, the *Spray* from Boston. On April 24, 1895, two months after his fifty-first birthday, Slocum set sail from Boston on his single-handed, three-year voyage around the world, a distance of forty-six thousand miles.

The *Spray*, measuring thirty-six feet, nine inches in length, had a beam of fourteen feet, two inches. Her draft was just over four feet. There was no engine or generator.

The *Spray* originated in a joke played on Slocum by a retired whaling captain. As the nineteenth century drew toward an end, steam was swiftly replacing sail as a means of nautical propulsion. Many of the tall sailing ships lay at dockside, their skeletal masts and yardarms stripped bare, waiting for the ship breakers or for cargoes that never come. Others had their masts removed and were towed about as coal barges. Hundreds of sailing ship masters found themselves stranded on the beach or retired to "old sailors" homes. Joshua Slocum, twenty-five years a sailing-ship captain, found himself beached. The ship owners no longer wanted the men who were instrumental in establishing the United States as one of the world's leading seafaring nations. Slocum spent his days browsing along the waterfronts, passing the time with watchmen aboard laid-up sailing hulks and talking with other unemployed captains. It was one of these old cronies who offered Slocum a ship that "wants some repairs." The ship was located at Fairhaven just opposite New Bedford. The vessel was Slocum's "for the taking—no strings attached."

The next day Slocum saw his "new" ship. He had been the butt of a hoax, for the *Spray* was an antiquated wreck whose age or origin none of the townsfolk could remember. She had been blocked up in a field several miles from the water for at least seven years. Being a resolute man and having little to do, Slocum accepted the prank as a challenge. The hulk required so much rebuilding that the many retired sea captains visiting with him during the eighteen months that he spent working on the boat couldn't tell whether the *Spray* was a new boat or an old vessel rebuilt. In addition to his own labor, Slocum spent $553.62 on materials to reincarnate the *Spray*.

Among those who knew the boat and the man, the big question was: Will it pay? The ship's sailing qualities were outstanding. The *Spray* could outspeed and outsail most other vessels anywhere near her size. It was only after an unsuccessful attempt at commercial fishing that Slocum decided to sail her alone around the world. There were many critics of the old captain's plan, for the feat had never been done before and was considered impossible.

But Slocum was not a man to be deterred—and he embarked on the voyage, a journey full of adventure, mystery and close calls. In his book, *Sailing Alone Around the World,* Slocum describes an incident near the Azores in which he fell seriously ill. As he lay doubled up in pain on the floor of the boat's cabin, a storm struck. But he was too sick and delirious to shorten sail.

He passed out. Sometime later he awakened. The gale was still blowing. Looking out the companionway, he saw, to his shock, a man at the helm holding the *Spray* on a steady course in spite of the sea's turbulence. The man, dressed in clothing of centuries past, introduced himself as a member of Columbus's crew, the pilot of the *Pinta*. He said he had come to guide Slocum's ship that night.

The next morning, after Slocum had recovered sufficiently to go out on deck, the gale was moderating and the sun was shining. The strange helmsman was nowhere to be seen. Everything on deck that hadn't been secured was washed away by the storm. The decks were whitened by the sunbaked salt spray. The gale had been more severe than Slocum had imagined. Yet the sails that he had been too sick to furl were still set and pulling, when they should have been ripped to shreds. Then he discovered that the *Spray* had made a good ninety miles right on course during the night. Only a skilled helmsman could make that happen.

Slocum had originally plotted his course from west to east—across the Atlantic, through the Mediterranean, Suez Canal, Red Sea, and into the Indian Ocean. Eventually, he would cross the Pacific, round Cape Horn, and sail up the Atlantic back to Boston. But these plans were thwarted by an attempted attack by Mediterranean pirates as he was approaching Gibralter. The *Spray* proved its sailing qualities by outrunning the Arab's dhow. Having been warned about the pirates in the Mediterranean and Red Seas, Slocum, after this encounter, decided to head back across the Atlantic and toward Cape Horn. His circumnavigation from east to west included run-ins with savages, storms, self-important customs agents and the like. In addition to his one-dollar alarm clock, which he used as a navigation timepiece because he didn't have the fifteen dollars to have his chronometer repaired, he had a compass, a sextant, and sailing charts.

When Slocum sailed the *Spray* into Boston Harbor on June 27, 1898, the fanfare was minimal. Only locally did the fifty-four-year-old sailor receive the honors he deserved for being the first person ever to sail alone around the world. The newspaper headlines were dominated by news of the Spanish-American War and the chain of American naval victories. Slocum's rise to fame was gradual as the war ended, but fame and glory did come to the old man and his old boat. His book not only became a bestseller but was required reading in many public schools. And this sailor, who couldn't swim a stroke, was in demand worldwide as a lecturer.

In between his writing, public appearances, and other activities, Slocum still managed to find time to sail the *Spray*. In the autumns of 1905, 1907, and 1908, he set sail from his home at West Tisbury on Martha's Vineyard to spend the winters cruising alone through the West Indies. His favorite port of call was Grand Cayman Island.

In the fall of 1909, Slocum, then sixty-five years old, set forth on another single-handed voyage to the Caribbean. On November 14, he was seen south of Cape Hatteras. Joshua Slocum, the greatest sailor of them all, and the *Spray* from Boston disappeared forever.

Today, after several hundred or more sailors have soloed around the world under sail, Joshua Slocum's name is still most often associated with that feat. During World War II, the United States Government honored Slocum when it launched the Liberty ship SS *Joshua Slocum*.

TWENTY-FIVE

Ghost Guard to the Rescue

D own through the years, there have been many reports of "ghost crews" saving both lives and vessels in distress. One, in the summer of 1978, involved
Bob Fowler, a sailor from West Palm Beach, Florida.
Fowler was attempting a single-handed transatlantic
crossing in an eighteen-foot sailboat, the *Miskeeter*.
When I met Bob, he looked more like a dockmaster at
a yacht club, or maybe a PR man on his day off. He
was typical of the yachtsmen in the pages of boating
magazines.

Fowler was using the 1978 transatlantic crossing as a
warm-up for an around-the-world voyage with the *Miskeeter* in the 1980s. He put to sea from Palm Beach on
June 10, 1978. It was a bright sunny day with only a
few scattered clouds. The sea was fairly calm. But the
fine sailing weather was not to last. During the first
night, while off Fort Pierce, Florida, a squall bore down
on the eighteen-foot sloop. "From then on," said Fowler,

"it was bad weather all the way. You might say I sailed from bad weather to worse weather.

"I was sailing the great circle route, and when I reached forty-four degrees north, WWV radio began warning of bad weather on the two northernmost Atlantic shipping routes. I made an effort to get as far south as possible, but since the *Miskeeter* has no auxiliary engine, I had made it only to about forty degrees north when the first of the really bad fronts caught me."

Winds and seas were quickly up to force nine, and gusts were as high as sixty knots. From then on, the voyage was a nightmare. The fifteen and twenty-foot seas looked fifty feet high from the cockpit of the eighteen-foot sailboat. All sails except the twenty-four square foot spitfire had been taken in, but still *Miskeeter* seemed to be under water as much as above it. Each breaking wave gave a hissing sound that ended with a reverberating boom against the boat. The wind screamed through the rigging. At times, the tiny vessel overrode a wave crest, and, for what seemed an eternity, the bottom of the world would fall out until a sudden crashing impact brought back the harsh reality of an environment gone mad.

Large ships that couldn't get far enough south to be out of the storm's path were having a rough time, too. But for Bob Fowler it was pure hell. He couldn't carry out neccessary bodily functions, couldn't eat, and was unable even to reach for a sip of water. He was hanging on for dear life. Never had he imagined that the sea could be so unpredictible.

No sleep, no food, no water—nothing but barely being able to hang on for dear life for four full days. "I lay strapped in my bunk in a state of constant apprehension, almost waiting to die as the seas crashed over my boat. I had done everything possible to secure the boat, and I had been awake for ninety hours. Exhaustion had obviously taken its toll, for then I saw them—three sailors, all wearing tan shirts and non-skid boating shoes. The sailors looked like anyone you'd see at a marina. I was so taken aback that I became oblivious to the aches and pains from all the bruises on my body, caused from being slammed about. Because of my state of fatigue, I knew I had to be hallucinating. I knew it had to be my imagination. I'm not a believer in the supernatural. It's very easy to see something that isn't there when you're exhausted, wet and hungry.

"Besides, I don't know how four of us could get into that little cabin. I just don't think that it was anything other than my imagination. Other lone-sailors have had the same experience when things got precarious at sea. They've all been through it. I've talked to a number of them. Really there's nothing supernatural or strange about it."

Fowler was quite sincere in his skepticism. Maybe his ordeal had caused his mind to play tricks on him. And, then again, maybe not.

"Then," said Fowler, "they began discussing among themselves the best storm tactics. 'Should we lay ahull, should we run with or without warps?' 'Don't run,' one of them advised. 'Her length is too short, and she'll pitch-pole.' 'Lay ahull and hold on,' another suggested. It seemed so real and clear. I couldn't recognize any of their faces. One of them said, 'We can't let him take the helm—he's too sleepy; and if he runs off before the wind, he'll kill us all.'

"They were mocking me and calling me a poor

sailor," Fowler continued. "One of them said, 'Push him, he's going to fall asleep.' It was just like having a nightmare, and you're trying to wake up and can't. Then one of the sailors said, 'Next time we sign on as crew, we'll make sure we don't get a sleepyhead.' "

Although Fowler kept restating his doubts as to the reality of the phantom crew, I got the feeling that deep down he hadn't totally convinced himself. The further the story progressed, the more intrigued I became.

"They kept mocking my seamanship. 'You didn't lash the tiller tight enough. It's come loose. Get up there and secure it before you lose the rudder! Go on, get topside!' I dragged myself on deck, and to my amazement, the tiller had come unlashed and was slapping from side to side. I relashed it, struggled back below, and collapsed in my bunk. But I couldn't sleep, because they kept at me. I begged and pleaded with them to leave me alone, but they kept on talking for what seemed like hours. 'Go check the battery, the cap's come off, and acid is leaking!' said one of them who was wearing a blue windbreaker. But I was too weak to move. And still they kept at me. I don't know which was worse, them or the storm.

"Hour after hour they nagged at me. Finally, they convinced me that I would never reach my destination, which was Plymouth, England. Then, to my astonishment, one of them said, 'Take your flare gun and go on deck. There's a ship out there.'

"With what seemed like the last of my strength, I managed to crawl out on deck with my flare gun. I couldn't believe what I saw—a ship in the distance. I fired off six flares in rapid succession.

"Within minutes the ship, the Finnish freighter M/V *Andrew*, bound for Baltimore with a cargo of newsprint, was alongside. But the seas were too high for them to take me and the *Miskeeter* aboard. The ship lay to, waiting for the seas to subside. I went back below. The three sailors who had been tormenting me were gone."

Some hours later, after being hove-to in the protective lee of the Finnish ship, Fowler and the *Miskeeter* were aboard the *Andrew*, en route to Baltimore.

When I interviewed Fowler at his office more than a year after his strange voyage, he was still convinced that his spectral shipmates were but figments of his imagination. But how does one account for the fact that the phantom sailors warned him about the tiller coming unlashed, told him that he'd never reach his destination, and alerted him to the passing ship?

One more thing: after being taken aboard the *Andrew*, Fowler slept for twelve hours. After awakening and taking some food, his first in more than four days, he examined the *Miskeeter*, which had been hoisted aboard the freighter and lashed down to the deck. When he opened the cockpit locker, he saw that one of the caps was missing from the battery, and acid had been leaking out of it. Although the locker had not been open during the storm, the missing battery cap was nowhere to be found.

Hallucinations, figments of the imagination, phantom sailors, or whatever the ghostly mariners were, the fact remains that they saved Robert Fowler and his little ship.

TWENTY-SIX

Seagoing Celebrities and Their Ghosts

One of the most famous nautical haunters is a Tasmanian adventurer who emigrated to the United States where he made and lost a fortune. Errol Leslie Thomon Flynn, better known as just plain Errol Flynn, always owned a yacht once he had climbed to stardom. There had been much controversy as to whether his yachts were used for fulfilling his lust for the sea or his lust for young women. Some of the wildest seagoing parties ever given were held aboard Flynn's yacht *Sirocco*.

During World War II, Flynn, the swashbuckling Hollywood "he-man," somehow managed to avoid military service. While American sailors were sacrificing their lives in the Pacific, Errol Flynn was also sailing the Pacific—between Los Angeles and Catalina, hosting orgies aboard the *Sirocco*. It was rumored that he bought his way out of the service. In real life, he was far from being the hero that he portrayed on the screen. Unlike other celebrities, Flynn never offered to entertain American servicemen, and he is said to have sold U.S. military information to both Nazi Germany and Japan.

After the war, *Sirocco* was sold. Flynn replaced it with a 118-foot, two-masted schooner named *Zaca*, which is Samoan for "peace." Just as *Sirocco* was best known for Flynn's drunken parties, *Zaca* soon became famous as the place where its owner seduced teenaged girls, for which he was arrested on a number of occassions.

Many famous movie stars, including John Barrymore, Alan Hale, David Niven, and Gary Cooper, had been guests aboard the *Zaca*. Flynn and Nora Eddington, the second of his three wives, spent their happiest moments aboard the schooner—until Nora discovered how many other women were also spending their happiest moments on the vessel.

Other celebrities such as Mary Pickford and Ali Khan had chartered the *Zaca*. Flynn's guests were often entertained by fights between him and various members of the crew. On one occassion, after a crewman engaged in a fight with the captain, the star picked up the luckless sailor and threw him overboard.

Flynn spent the last happy moments of his life aboard the *Zaca* with sixteen-year-old Beverly Aadland, the last of his many loves. Toward the end, Flynn, quite ill and in financial straits, moved the *Zaca* up the coast from Los Angeles to Vancouver to prevent it from falling into the hands of the Internal Revenue Service.

Badly in need of money, Flynn decided that the *Zaca* should be sold. On October 14, 1959, a Vancouver couple who were in the process of buying the *Zaca*, invited Flynn and Beverly to a party. It was still early evening when Flynn said, "I think I'll lie down. I shall return."

In a hallway leading to the hosts' bedroom, Flynn collapsed from a massive heart attack. The fifty-year-old actor was dead on arrival at the hospital. A coronor's report stated that Flynn had died as the result of a coronory thrombosis complicated by hardening of the arteries, degeneration of the liver, and an infection of the lower intestine. Errol Flynn's body was that of a very old man.

The corpse was shipped back to California on a freight train. Just before the funeral, a film director friend of Flynn's sneaked a dozen bottles of whiskey into the star's casket. Friends agreed that he would have appreciated the gesture. However, he would not have been very happy to have known that most of the people with whom he had worked in films found excuses not to attend his funeral.

A marker was never placed over Errol Flynn's grave.

Beverly Aadland never became a movie star as Flynn had promised her. Her life took a darker, more mysterious turn—although one just as dramatic. A short time after Flynn's death, a man was found shot to death in her bedroom. The coroner ruled it suicide.

Flynn's parents, both residing in England at the time of his death, died shortly thereafter—his father as the result of a stroke, his mother in a car accident.

Sean, Flynn's only son, became a well-known news photographer. Young Flynn acted in real life the role that his father had played in the movies. He went to Vietnam as a correspondent and disappeared while covering an assignment during a jungle battle. He was listed as missing and presumed dead.

The *Zaca* was sold, and the new owner sailed it to Europe. During the passage, Errol Flynn's personal flag—a question mark against a plain background—flew from the mast. Before the return cruise began, the *Zaca*, almost as if in a gesture of defiance, broke down as Flynn's flag waved in the wind high above the deck. It was towed to a shipyard at the French Riviera, where it lay rotting away for years.

But those years of disintegration were not years of inactivity. A number of witnesses reported seeing Flynn's specter pacing the decks of the vessel. Most often, the actor's apparition was seen between sunset and dark. One watchman saw the ghost, jumped overboard, and was in a complete state of shock when pulled from the water.

A skipper of a vessel moored near the late actor's yacht also witnessed some strange goings-on aboard the *Zaca*. "One night there was music coming from the *Zaca*. You could hear girls' voices and laughter, and the lights on board were going on and off," he said. "It was as though a wild party was going on. But there couldn't have been a party, because no one was aboard. There wasn't even any electricity on her. Something strange was going on."

Could it be that the disturbed spirit of Errol Flynn seeks in death the happiness that he was never able to find in life?

In the mid-1970s, the owners of the shipyard where the rotting hulk of the *Black Witch* lay (as the *Zaca* is sometime called) decided to restore the 118-foot vessel. But there was one problem—Flynn's ghost.

Thus, it was decided to hold an exorcism to banish the late movie actor's ghost. A thirty-inch-long model of the *Zaca* to be used for the rite was taken to a Monte Carlo church on December 18, 1978, by a boat painter who had seen the apparition while working on the yacht. Others who had seen the ghost were also present. Conducting the service were an Anglican archdeacon and a Catholic priest.

As the ritual began, the archdeacon removed some salt from a glass container and uttered, "I exorcise thee, O creature of salt, by our living God. Let the spirit of pestilence abide here no more, nor the breath of moral perversion. Let every unclean spirit fly hence." As the archdeacon's chant echoed through the incense-laden air of the church, the boat painter let out a low moan and slumped forward in his pew as though possessed. Within a few minutes, he seemed all right again.

The archdeacon went on, "Send the holy angels from Heaven above to protect and cherish all those who go aboard this ship. Let the *Zaca* be hallowed. Let cheer, joy and health be given to all aboard *Zaca*. Deliver this vessel and all who board her from evil." The ritual lasted twenty minutes.

Afterward, the priest said, "I am positive that the spirits of evil have departed, and the peace of God should be with the boat. I prayed from my heart for Errol Flynn, for I remember his face. I hope that he may enter the kingdom of God, where he may find eternal peace."

Everyone who participated in the ceremony felt that it was a success. But they didn't take into account that it had been held in a church rather than aboard the *Zaca* and that Errol Flynn would never have been caught dead in a church.

How can one be sure that Flynn's ghost no longer roams the decks of the *Zaca*? Very simply—just spend a night aboard the vessel—alone.

• • •

Aside from being movie stars, Errol Flynn and John Wayne had little in common. Wayne was greatly admired and respected by his peers. He was a hero. Flynn was a self-admitted rogue. However, both of them loved the sea. While *Zaca* was but one of a score of Flynn's mistresses, the *Wild Goose* was John Wayne's only mistress.

The *Wild Goose* was an ex–United States Navy minesweeper built of heavy wood and about 135 feet long. Her hull design made her one of the most seaworthy warships of her size. The YMS's, as the navy designated them, often reached an invasion site well ahead of the landing fleet. Their war record was sterling.

Just a few weeks before his death, John Wayne sold the *Wild Goose* to a Santa Monica attorney (name witheld on request).

Some people who have been aboard the *Wild Goose* since the superstar's demise have felt his presence. A reporter wrote, "John Wayne is dead. But his 'True Grit' spirit still walks the decks of his beloved yacht, the *Wild Goose*."

"I feel he [Wayne] is on board everywhere I look," said the new owner. "Sometimes when I'm in his stateroom, sleeping in his bed, I wake up at two or three in the morning knowing that his presence is there."

I asked the new owner if he'd ever had any experience other than just a feeling. He replied, "A guest, who was spending the night aboard the *Wild Goose*, got up about three in the morning and noticed the shadowy figure of a man standing about ten feet away in the darkness. Thinking it was me standing there, my guest addressed the form. The figure's reaction was to back off into the darkness and disappear. My guest rushed to the porthole of the master stateroom and looked in at me. I was sound asleep in John Wayne's custom-built king-sized bed. There was no way that I could have made it into the stateroom before my guest reached the porthole. There was no one else aboard at the time."

Later, when the guest described the incident, the owner asked what the stranger looked like. The apparition was too tall to have been the owner, a member of the crew, or anyone else who could possibly have boarded the vessel that night. The figure appeared to be about six feet, four inches tall and to weigh about 225 pounds—very close to the "Duke's" physique.

The owner mentioned that on occasion, he would return to the ship after several days ashore to find that someone had been lying in John Wayne's bad. There would be an impression in the mattress, an impression well over six feet long.

When I mentioned the then recent exorcism rites associated with Errol Flynn's yacht, the new owner said, "Never on this ship. As far as I am concerned, it's a friendly spirit that we have here. And if indeed it is John Wayne's spirit, he's welcome aboard."

The new owner went on to tell me about a strange incident concerning some of the lamps aboard the ship. "I went to a place that sold used nautical equipment and bought some brass hurricane lamps that I thought were quite rare and unusual looking and would look good on the galley bulkhead. After they were put up, the ship's engineer walked into the galley, saw the lanterns and said, 'I took those lights down years ago and stashed them away below. John Wayne had me take them down because he was always bumping his head on them.' The engineer was even more surprised when I told him that I had bought the lamps. Did somebody steal and sell them? We went below to where the original lamps had been stowed. They were still there and were identical to the ones I had bought. These are very unusual looking lights, and the chances of finding matching ones would be something like one in ten thousand.

"I left the hurricane lamps hanging in the galley. That night, I had difficulty falling asleep. When I finally did doze off, it wasn't for long. I woke up about three in the morning, and the presence of John Wayne in the master stateroom was very strong. Never before had I felt his presence that much. John Wayne was there, I knew it. I got up to walk around, and it were as if he were following me wherever I went."

John Wayne had grown up around boats and was one of the few Hollywood celebrities who could run his own yacht. Although he had done a lot of sailing, he still considered himself a powerboat man. He was as good a seaman off the screen as he was a cowboy or cavalryman on the screen. During a North Atlantic crossing, the *Wild Goose* encountered a violent gale. The vessel was rolling as much as forty-five degrees. The crew, most of them seasick, were huddled below decks praying. Wayne managed to get about half of them topside. But some of them, fearing the *Wild Goose* might founder, went back below. With almost no assistance, the "Duke" guided his ship safely through the storm.

John Wayne was a believer in life after death. His favorite drinking toast was, "May you live forever . . . and the last voice you hear be mine."

After Wayne's death, his estranged wife said, "I

would have done anything, even given my own life, to bring him back." Maybe John Wayne, superstar, super patriot and super sailor is back . . . aboard the *Wild Goose*.

TWENTY-SEVEN

Ghosts on the Mississippi

Not all events involving maritime ghosts happen on the high seas or in harbors boardering the oceans. Incidents relating to nautical manifestations have taken place hundreds of miles inland from the sea. There is a stretch of the Mississippi River in the areas of Natchez, Vicksburg, and St. Joseph where strange things have happened—and are still happening. The region abounds with Indian lore of spirits and the supernatural.

At certain times, weird, hysterical screams are heard coming from the middle of the river. The cries sound like the voice of a woman. They are followed by the French words, *"Gaston! Gaston! Aidez-moi au nom de Dieu! Les hommes me blessent!"* ("Gaston! Help me in the name of God! The men are hurting me!") People living in the area who've heard the screams believe that they have something to do with the river steamer *Iron Mountain*, and its unknown fate nearly a hundred and twenty-five years ago.

The *Iron Mountain* was a large Mississippi paddle-wheel steamer that plied the Mississippi and Ohio Rivers between New Orleans and Pittsburgh after the Civil War. Those vessels were like floating towns with their own theatrical groups, gamblers, musicians, prostitutes, and various other diversions.

The *Iron Mountain* was in excess of 180 feet in length, with a beam of thirty-five feet. In addition to carrying passengers, she towed freight barges. The vessel's calliope could be heard long before the smoke from her belching stacks could be seen as she approached various towns of call. And wherever she called, a holiday atmosphere reigned.

In June 1874, the *Iron Mountain* cast off from her wharf at Vicksburg and set off for New Orleans. She was carrying fifty-seven passengers and towing a string of barges. As she reached midstream and approached a bend, the pilot gave a long blast on the steamboat's whistle. The *Iron Mountain* rounded the bend and was never seen again.

The barges were found with the tow ropes cut clean through. No trace of wreckage from the big steamer or dead bodies were ever found. The paddle steamer *Iron Mountain* had simply vanished. Hundreds of miles of river bottom in both directions were dragged without success.

Other riverboats steaming upstream should have passed the *Iron Mountain*. None reported seeing her. Except for a few deep holes that were thoroughly dredged, there was no water deep enough to completely cover the huge vessel. Had she been wrecked or burned, there would have been bodies and debris. There appears to be no earthly explanation for the disappearance of the *Iron Mountain*.

Although not one shred of evidence revealing the fate of the big riverboat or its passengers was ever found, local people feel that the spirit of one of its passengers is still around and might someday give a clue as to what happened just south of Vicksburg.

Many theories have been formulated, but only one seems to be more than conjecture. Because river pirates still prowled the waters of the Mississippi in the years following the Civil War, some local people think that the *Iron Mountain* was captured by these pirates who, after an orgy of rape and killing, buried the bodies, dismantled the steamer and secreted the sections where they would never be found.

Eleven months after the *Iron Mountain* disappeared forever, another palatial Mississippi River paddle-wheel vessel, the *Mississippi Queen*, cast off from Memphis on April 17, 1873. Like the ill-fated *Iron Mountain*, her destination was New Orleans. She was last seen shortly before midnight, about twelve hours after her departure. Then she, too, vanished without a trace down on the Mississippi River.

TWENTY-EIGHT

Phantom Vessels

Although some ships, like the *Houston* and the *Stewart*, have been called "ghosts" or "ghost ships" in a joking sort of way, what about a real ghost ship or phantom of the sea?

Take the case of the spectral square-rigged sailing ship that plies her way to her fiery doom almost every year either just before or right after the sun's autumnal equinox over Nova Scotia.

Merigomash is a small fishing village located on Nova Scotia's north shore, south of Prince Edward Island near where the Northumberland Strait joins the Gulf of Saint Lawrence. It is just offshore from Merigomash where the phantom vessel appears. In the early part of December 1953, according to the Associated Press, hundreds of people observed the specter ship making almost nightly manifestations.

As each autumn turns into winter, shore dwellers keep a regular vigil for the strange wraith. When it appears, phones ring, and roads become jammed with folks rush-

ing down to the wooded shore to witness the unbelievable.

As the ship moves into view on a northeasterly course,
with every rag of canvas her three masts can carry, a
deathlike silence reigns over the crowd of spectators
who cannot believe what they are seeing. Why does she
move so fast, even when no wind is blowing? And if
there is fog or haze, her outline glows as though phos-
phorescent. Those running along the shore on foot or
horseback cannot keep up with her.

Soon, ominous lights appear to be moving along her
heeling decks. Then, suddenly, the phantom vessel shud-
ders as though she has run aground. Shadowy forms are
racing along her length. But before any of them reach
their goal, the vessel is engulfed in flames. Burning top
masts and yardarms crash to her decks. Obscure figures
begin to jump over her sides. Then, as the spectral ship
becomes engulfed in flames from stem to stern, she
plunges bow-first down into the black waters—and the
night is black once again.

The ghost ship with its phantom crew has been in-
triguing Nova Scotians for well over two hundred years.
Although the identity of the vessel is unknown, most
natives of the area believe it to be a pirate ship that went
down with all hands in those straits.

Is there really a ghost ship that plies the waters south
of Prince Edward Island each December? Or could it be
that hundreds of God-fearing people are hallucinating?
Then, maybe, it is a time warp that has never been able
to escape the confines of earth. Another possibility could
be that the deeds of the pirate crew were so blasphe-
mous, that they've been condemned to relive their deaths
on each anniversary. Who knows?

TWENTY-NINE

The Phantom of the *Forrestal*

In 1998 and 1999, the United States Navy issued an inventory of retired, surplus ships that were available for museums, patriotic monuments, or historic display. One of those ships is moored at Newport, where before the fog lifts on a chilly Rhode Island morning, her masthead and parts of her superstructure loom up out of the morning mist like some long-dormant prehistoric creature. Though she is crewless and unmanned, there is no rest between her decks.

Other listed vessels, mothballed at various bases, include the battleship USS *New Jersey* at Bremerton (now donated to her namesake state) and the aircraft carrier USS *Midway*. Among other craft are cruisers, destroyers, frigates, and an ancient tug left over from the 1941 attack on Pearl Harbor. The ship at Newport, however, the aircraft carrier USS *Forrestal*, differs from the others in one particular respect. All the other ships are painted a faded battleship gray with some black trim. Their names and numbers are still mostly visible. So, how does the *Forrestal* differ?

Whereas the others are totally lifeless, the *Forrestal* rustles with shipboard activity. And though her last crewmen has been long ago reassigned to other stations or ships, and its bridge and hanger decks and engine room and passageways no longer echo to the footsteps of sailors answering their call to quarters—life, or rather afterlife, still goes on aboard the big flattop.

The *Forrestal*'s keel was put down in 1952. Named after a former secretary of the navy, she was commissioned on October 1, 1956, three years too late for the Korean War. Her greatest distinction, however, was that she was the first aircraft carrier anywhere to be built after the end of World War II. She was also distinguished as having been the earliest flattop designed and built specifically to operate jet aircraft. Her hull was structurally compartmentized to reduce the effects of both conventional and nuclear attack, an innovation that would one day prove fatal. Unlike her predecessors, the bow under her flight deck was enclosed to improve her seakindliness. Her plated armored flight deck, the length of three and a half football fields, was angled so that parked aircraft would not interfere with others taking off or landing. The navy designed the *Forrestal* to rectify all of the weaknesses of her World War II predecessors. Although she did serve in the Viet Nam area, the *Forrestal* never experienced direct action or attack by an enemy. Her planes and aircrews did participate in air combat, but her highly advanced and innovative combat design was never actually put to test. But since the *Forrestal* was a ship of such huge proportions, she did have her quota of fatal mishaps.

As previously mentioned, strange sounds and sightings have been reported aboard the deactivated *Forrestal*. However, those goings-on have nothing to do with the ship's dormancy. Bizzare events were reported aboard even while she was on active sea duty with her full complement of 148 officers and 2810 enlisted men.

During the big flattop's final years of active service, crewmen reported numerous incidents that were beyond any logical explanation. Secured hatches opened mysteriously and slammed in cadence with the rhythm from each roll of the ship; unfamiliar voices were heard over disconnected intercom phones; lights came on by themselves; and eerie sounds were emitted from unoccupied compartments. And, of course, there was the seeing of the unseen.

During a six-month tour of the Indian Ocean and Arabian Gulf near the end of her career, Lieutenant James Brooks, the carrier's public relations officer was quoted as saying, "Whoever, or whatever it is, crew members swear a ghost is responsible for flickering lights, voices on disconnected telephones and things that go bump in the night.

"Incredibly," he added, "some of the men claim they've even seen a ghost prowling below decks."

Far below the ship's waterline are two compartments that sailors had become hesitant to enter. The spaces were originally designed as mammoth cold storage lockers for her enormous crew. Ironically, though, on July 29, 1967, her flight and hanger decks were encased by fire and explosion as her Skyhawks were being fueled with JT-5 jet fuel in the Gulf of Tonkin off North Vietnam. Although it never was officially admitted, the fire and explosions resulted from a succession of human errors.

Bodies and body parts of the 137 crewmen who perished in the fiery catastrophe were stowed in the deep freezers, which had been transformed into temporary morgues. Thus, some of the crew theorized that the *Forrestal*'s ghost is the restless spirit of a petty officer killed in that fire while sealed in one of the ship's combat-proof battle compartments. Others believe the spirit is a pilot who perished in a previous crash, for several sightings had been reported before the 1967 tragedy.

The apparitions definitely were not hallucinations beheld by a handful of superstitious sailors. Petty Officer Dan Balboa, who was in charge of the officer's mess, claimed that for years after the disaster, some of his men refused to go alone into those two compartments, deep down in the bowels of the ship, which were again being used for frozen food. One crewman actually became demented whenever he neared the area. On the verge of panic, the ship's cook, absolutely and adamantly, refused to go anywhere near the freezer compartments. He had to be transferred off the ship. "I've never seen the ghost myself, but I know that guy saw the ghost of someone he once knew," added Balboa. "But I've sure heard some strange sounds from down there.

"One night I was taking inventory down there, and I repeatedly heard the sound of a heavy steel deck grating being lifted and slammed back down. Yet, each time I turned around, there was nothing there, and the noise stopped."

Balboa went on, "Once when I was down there checking the temperature of the food freezers, freezer doors I had shut and latched kept popping open. I was alone down there."

Sighting or sounds of the ship's ghost became so commonplace that the vessel's crew named the spirit "George." Second Class Cook James Hillard said, "I've seen George myself. I still get goose bumps when I think about it. Most eerie was when I was working in the galley one day, and I looked out into the passageway. I saw him—a ghostlike figure wearing a khaki uniform like a chief or officer. He passed less than six feet from me and looked like a real person, but I could see right through him. He walked right through a closed door into a food storage room."

Another petty officer, Gary Weiss, also claimed to have seen "George." "I saw him, clad in khaki, opening a hatch and descending down into one of the reefer compressor rooms. I climbed down the ladder after him, and there was no one there. That hatch was the only way in or out of that machinery space."

Other sailors have reported being touched or even grasped by a hand that "wasn't there." Some heard footsteps following them, but when they stopped and turned around, no one was there.

Hillard admitted that "George" had sort of become accepted as a shipmate by some of the crew, and they'd become used to his antics.

The majority of those who served with "George" aboard the USS *Forrestal* theorized that he was one of the 137 sailors who burned to death in the 1967 accident on the flight deck. Others believe that "George" is the ghost of the first pilot killed in a crash landing aboard the vessel.

There are others with a completely different belief, one that defies the imagination. A small group of sailors believe that the phantom of the *Forrestal* is the specter of none other than the carrier's namesake, James V. Forrestal, who once served as a navy pilot during the early biplane days of naval aviation. Eventually, through the right contacts, he was appointed as secretary of the navy in 1944 and served at that post until 1947, when he became the United States' first secretary of defense.

Eventually, James Forrestal met his end under exceptionally baffling circumstances, during a stay in a naval hospital where he was supposedly recovering from a nervous breakdown. He either fell, jumped, or was, as some of the carrier's crew believed, thrown from the window of his sixth-floor room. Did he make any enemies during his years in politics? Or could it be that he knew more than he should have known of certain skeltons in certain closets?

In November of 1999, I attended a dinner meeting of the Fort Lauderdale Navy League. The main speaker was Rear Admiral Mark Fitzgerald, USN, Deputy Commander U.S. Naval Forces, Central Command. During his speech, the admiral told of the different ships that he had served aboard during his career. When he mentioned the USS *Forrestal*, I knew that I had to talk to him.

After the meeting, I corralled him as he was heading for his car. When I asked him if he had ever heard of the ghosts aboard the *Forrestal,* his face lit up.

"Certainly," he replied. "I never saw any of them myself. But they were always one of the main topics in the wardroom."

I asked if there were any consensus among those who had served on the carrier as to whose spirits they might be. He mentioned several possibilities, including the victims of the 1966 flight deck mishap. Then as he walked off, he turned and said, "My guess would be the ship's namesake, the former secretary of the navy."

• • •

There is one man alive today who, more than anyone else, may know who "George," the phantom of the flat-top, really is. That man was sitting in his plane on the *Forrestal*'s flight deck waiting to take off on July 29, 1967. As he braced himself for launch, he felt the shock of an enormous blast from behind. A bomb had detached from another aircraft on deck, setting off an explosion. A piece of flaming shrapnel ripped through the gas tank of his Skyhawk. Momentarily stunned by the impact, he still managed to slip out of his safety harness. Then, blindly clawing and grappling his way out of the smoke-filled cockpit, the young pilot leaped to the blazing flight deck beneath the flame-engulfed Skyhawk. About to flee the hell raging across the flight deck, he hesitated. Then, with no concern for his own safety, he turned and, charging into the holocaust, began pulling stunned and wounded sailors from the inferno. One hundred and thirty-five of his shipmates perished in the mishap. The young pilot survived. His name: John McCain, future U.S. senator from Arizona and contender for the Republican party presidential nomination in the year 2000.

As of this writing, the USS *Forrestal* had been recently donated to Tampa, Florida, as a national monument. When the big carrier enters the Port of Tampa after its long tow down the eastern seaboard from Newport, Rhode Island, it will be greeted by thousands of small boats and yachts, fireboats and tugs with their water cannons streaking the sky, coast guard cutters and every other imaginable kind of nautical conveyance. But before the USS *Forrestal* can open for sight-seeing tours, an important question must be taken under consideration. *Where is "George"?*

THIRTY

The Death Ships

O f all the oceans on the face of the earth, one stands
above the others as a place of mystery and intrigue. Although it was one of the first offshore bodies
to be traveled on by civilized man, we know compara-
tively little about the Indian Ocean. Some hydrographers
claim that if there are still islands to be discovered, they
will be found in the Indian Ocean. This vast body of
water, which includes the Arabian Sea, the Bay of Bengal, the Timor Sea, the Java Sea, the Andaman Sea, the
South China Sea, the Tasman Sea, and other exotically
named bodies of water, extends from the east coast of
Africa to Indonesia and the Philippines, and south from
the sweltering Persian Gulf to the ice fields of Antarc-
tica.

The romantic names of her port cities—Kuala Lum-
pur, Djakarta, Rangoon, Zanzibar, Karachi, Columbo,
and hundreds of others—are deceptive. For instead of
resembling Rudyard Kipling's description of them in
"Mandalay," they teem with graft, corruption, disease,

terrorism, deceit, revolution, hunger, and maybe death for those who are not careful.

Like many of its port cities, the Indian Ocean has been a place where death and terror prevailed. Even today, it is the last bastion of piracy.

The waters of the Indian Ocean undoubtedly support more forms of deadly and voracious sea life than any other ocean—the ferocious estaurine crocodile, deadly sea snakes, killer sharks, and species not yet named. The Indian Ocean and its adjacent waters also host more than the average share of strange and unexplainable happenings, some of which have already been depicted in previous chapters of this book. But there are others.

In February 1948, a number of ships picked up a distress signal originating from the eastern part of the Bay of Bengal, near the Andaman Sea. The SOS was from the Dutch freighter SS *Ourang Medan* in the Malacca Strait. The *Ourang Medan* had been bound for Djakarta, Indonesia. Windless and flat calm, the sea appeared to be covered with oil. The sun appeared as an enormous fiery ball in the eastern sky. And as it climbed, so did the temperature.

The Dutch ship continued transmitting distress signals. "All officers, including captain, dead. Lying in chart room in bridge. Possibly whole crew dead." There were broken and distorted signals followed by, "I die!" Then silence. Rescue ships began homing in on the signal.

Within a few hours of the original signal, the first rescue vessel arrived on the scene. From a distance the *Ourang Medan* appeared to be dead in the water but not in any immediate danger. However, there was no response to hand and whistle signals. Radio signals went unanswered. A boat was launched, and a boarding party was on its way across the quarter mile that separated the two ships. As the boarders climbed over the *Ourang Medan*'s rail, everything appeared, at first, to be in order. It was only when they began to walk around the decks that they made a ghastly discovery. They were on a ship of death, a floating morgue.

A number of bodies, crew and officers alike, were found around the decks. Their eyes were open in an empty stare at the blazing sun. Their outstretched arms, frozen in rigor mortis, reached toward the blazing sun. Even the ship's dog was found dead, its face contorted in an eternal snarl. The captain's corpse was found in the wheelhouse. In the radio shack, the boarders found the radio operator slumped over his desk with one hand stretched toward the radio transmitting key. He may have been the last to die, for rigor mortis hadn't set in yet. His head rocked from side to side with each roll of the ship. It was the same down in the engine and fire rooms—all dead. All machinery had been stopped, and the boiler fires were out. The steam gauges showed less than ten pounds of pressure remaining. Each time the rescuers pointed a flashlight at a dead fireman or oiler, they would feel a chill, even though the temperature down there was 110 degrees. Not one body aboard the ship showed any sign of violence or injury.

A complete check of the ship disclosed nothing that might have caused the death of the crew. Aside from the boarding party, the only thing still alive around the *Ourang Medan* were the sharks swimming endlessly around the wallowing freighter as if they knew it was a ship of the dead.

It was decided to tow the ship to the nearest port.

Tackle was readied and a towline rigged between the ships. Just as a strain was about to be taken on the towline, smoke began pouring from one of the *Ourang Medan*'s holds. Unable to control the fire without steam to operate the fire and flushing pumps, the salvors fled back to their own ship.

Within minutes, the *Ourang Medan* was ripped open by a violent explosion, barely giving those aboard the towing ship a chance to cut the towline. Seconds later, the Dutch freighter slid beneath the surface, taking with her all the evidence as to what had made her a ship of the dead.

There was much speculation as to what might have happened to the *Ourang Medan*—toxic fumes from the cargo, food poisoning, South China Sea pirates, disease. But as one Indonesian official said, "Maybe it's better that we don't know what happened to that ship and its crew."

Five years to the month after the *Ourang Medan* incident, another strange report came from out of the Indian Ocean. On February 7, 1953, the British cargo ship *Ranee*, owned by the Asiatic Steam Navigation Company, was plying the waters between Nicobar and the Andaman Islands in the Bay of Bengal. The *Ranee*'s lookout sighted an apparently disabled ship wallowing aimlessly in the windless sea. As the *Ranee* closed the distance between the two ships, the lookout read the name on the vessel's bow: *Holchu*. The *Ranee* attempted to communicate with the *Holchu* by radio and whistle signals but received no response. A boarding party was sent over to the *Holchu*.

Once aboard the heaving ship, the boarders found the

vessel deserted. In the galley, they discovered a meal already prepared but cold and beginning to turn moldy. Apparently whatever happened to the crew took place before that day, for the meal was the crew's breakfast. The ship was found to be seaworthy; it had plenty of fuel and provisions and gave no clue as to why it had been deserted.

The *Holchu* was towed to port, where an official examination, including a scrutinization of the vessel from stem to stern, failed to disclose any reason why the crew left the ship. Even though calm seas had prevailed for days, no trace of the missing crew was ever found. The peril of the sea that the *Holchu* encountered remains another mystery of the Indian Ocean.

Numerous vessels have been found in the Indian Ocean and its adjacent seas under circumstances similar to those of the *Holchu*.

Only an authenticated sighting of the legendary "Flying Dutchman" could be more startling than the episode experienced by the crew of the SS *Khosrou* in the Indian Ocean in January 1937.

The story really began on January 5, 1931. The 442-foot Norwegian motorship *Tricolor* (some sources spell it *Tricoleur*) was en route from Oslo and various North Sea ports to Yokohama, Japan, with a general cargo consisting mostly of chemical products. The *Tricolor* had unloaded some cargo during a stopover at Columbo, Ceylon, and was on the final leg of her voyage to Japan. She would never reach her destination. In fact, she got only four miles beyond the sea buoy at Columbo when she was ripped open amidship by a tremendous explosion. The 6,000-ton ship was immediately engulfed in flames from stem to stern. Within five minutes, the *Tricolor* sank. Thirty-six of the forty-two persons on board were rescued from life rafts and floating debris by the French liner *Porthos*. Among the missing was the *Tricolor*'s captain, Arthur Wold.

On December 20, 1936, the second part of the *Tricolor* mystery began to unfold. On that day, almost five years after the *Tricolor* blew up, the *Khosrou* departed Calcutta for Bombay. Just behind the *Khosrou* was the SS *Maimyo*, also bound for Bombay. The weather was overcast, a steady drizzle was falling, and visibility was less than a mile as the two vessels headed out to sea.

A week later, the *Khosrou* was off the coast of Ceylon. It was 0200 (2:00 A.M.), and the third officer, G. E. Robinson, was in charge of the watch. The captain, who had retired to his cabin at midnight, suddenly burst into the wheelhouse shouting, "The ship is in danger of running aground! Get someone to take a sounding!"

"But, sir, we're right on course," responded the third officer.

"Take a sounding anyway," replied the captain. "I just had a horrible nightmare that we ran aground." A sounding was taken, and it indicated that the ship was in less than 13 fathoms (seventy-eight feet) of water. The course was abruptly changed toward deeper water.

A minute later, the radio operator came rushing into the wheelhouse and told the captain, "Just picked up a message from the *Maimyo*, she ran aground at exactly 0200."

With the dawn's first light, the *Maimyo*, hard aground, appeared just within range of *Khosrou*'s visibility. She had run onto an uncharted shoal. "You know," said the *Khosrou*'s captain, "I dreamt that we sailed from Calcutta for Bombay just like we really did, and it was raining all the time like it is now. Then we ran aground, and that woke me. It seemed so real. And the time, too. Two A.M. Just when the *Maimyo* ran aground. That's quite a coincidence, isn't it?"

After seeing that the crew of the *Maimyo* was all right, the *Khosrou* continued on to Bombay. From there, her orders were to return to Calcutta. Although it was the dry season, the monsoonlike rain continued. The *Khosrou* was steaming along at under five knots. Visibility was less than a mile. At one-minute intervals, a seaman was sounding a siren as a warning to any other ship that may be just beyond the *Khosrou*'s range of visibility.

Somewhere out in the mist and rain there was another ship—an approaching ship, for her siren signals were getting louder. The *Khosrou*'s engine was stopped, and she drifted slowly ahead. Each blast of her siren was answered by the other ship. Suddenly, the other vessel appeared, ghostlike, out of the mist, dead ahead. Had the *Khosrou* not stopped her engine when she did, the two ships would have collided.

The other vessel was estimated as being no less than 5,000 tons. As she crossed his ship's bow, Robinson trained his glasses on the vessel. Scanning the ship from the bow aft, he saw no one on deck. Training his binoculars on the bridge, he saw that it, too, was deserted. But he did observe the ship's name painted on the trailboard secured to the bridge: *Tricolor*. A number of blasts of the *Khosrou*'s whistle failed to bring anyone out onto the *Tricolor*'s decks.

As the *Tricolor* disappeared into the gloom, the rain stopped. Within minutes, the afternoon sun began to break through the overcast sky. For the first time in days, the visibility became near perfect. But where was the *Tricolor*? She should have been no more than a mile or two away. But the sea was empty except for the coastline of Ceylon off in the distance. The officers took turns with the glasses, scanning from horizon to horizon, but there was no sign of the other ship.

As the captain took a bearing on the *Khosrou*'s position, Robinson came out of the chart room unrolling a chart on which to pinpoint the ship's exact location. The mate pointed to a symbol on the chart denoting a submerged wreck. Next to the symbol, the chart read, "*Tricolor*, sunk by explosion, 1700, Jan. 5, 1931."

"Today's January 5," stammered the captain. Just then there were two rings of the ship's bell announcing that it was 5:00 P.M., or 1700.

The chief mate came out of the wheelhouse with the ship's logbook. "Look here, Captain," he said, "this is the exact location where we thought we were running aground last week. Our sounding lead must have landed right on top of the wreck, because the chart shows the water as being thirty fathoms, and we got a reading of less than thirteen fathoms."

As for the ship with the name *Tricolor* that the men on the bridge of the *Khosrou* saw six years to the day and at the exact hour of the 1931 explosion, it could have been a coincidence. There might have been another ship named *Tricolor* heading into Columbo at the time of the sighting. A later check of the records, however, revealed that no other vessel with the name *Tricolor* was in the Indian Ocean at all during 1935 or 1936. Did the men aboard the *Khosrou* imagine what they saw? Did they hallucinate? Or did they really see a ghost ship that appears over its watery grave on the anniversary of its loss?

THIRTY-ONE

The Southern Oceans

In its November 13, 1913 issue, the *Wellington Post* in New Zealand carried an astonishing news report that sounded more like fiction than fact. Yet it was very true, according to the publication. The story actually began twenty-three years earlier.

Some of the most bizarre stories of the sea are occurrences in the southern ocean near Cape Horn. One of the most uncanny of those happenings involved the 1,200-ton sailing vessel *Marlborough*, a square rigger that vanished while en route from New Zealand to London in 1890. Although it was farther than sailing around the Horn of Africa, the square riggers preferred sailing from east to west to take advantage of the prevailing winds of the "roaring forties" and the south Atlantic. Timewise, it was faster. Under the command of Captain Hird, the *Marlborough* carried a crew of twenty-nine and one passenger when she sailed from Lyttelton, New Zealand, on January 11, which was midsummer in the southern hemisphere. Her cargo consisted of frozen meat and wool. Two days out, the 228-foot ship was sighted and spoken to by another vessel. That was supposedly the last ever seen of the *Marlborough*.

There are two different versions as to what fate may have befallen the *Marlborough*, a pioneering version of a refrigeration ship. C. Fox Smith, in *There Was a Ship*, relates the story of survivors from the bark *Cordova*, which was wrecked on July 23, 1890, on Tierra del Fuego near Cape Horn. None of the *Cordova*'s crew was lost, but they had to endure considerable suffering from exposure and hunger. The survivors formed several expeditions to set out in various directions in search of food and help.

Two of the men, according to Smith, made their way to Good Success Bay, a place where whaling ships had put in at one time. The two started their trek at daybreak, which was about 10:00 A.M. (it was then winter in the southern hemisphere). Soon they happened upon the hulk of a wrecked bark named *Godiva*. Only the aft half of the ship remained, and little was left of that. Apparently she had been carrying a cargo of coal, for a considerable amount of it was strewn about the area. After examining the wreckage and inventorying the salvageable items they would return for, the two men continued their journey. Several miles further along the shoreline, they discovered "a square sterned gig (a ship's boat) with teakwood thwarts." Painted on the boat's stern was "*Marlborough*, London." A short distance from the gig they discovered the shredded remains of a tent made from an old sail. Inside the tent, they found seven skeletons. Unaware of the *Marlborough*'s disappearance, the two men never returned to the site. Thirty-three days later, they and their shipmates were rescued by the German bark *Banca Mobilirio*.

When the *Marlborough*'s owners in London received word of the discovery of the gig and the grisly remains in the tent, they questioned the two men who had found them. "There is no doubt," said the owners, "that the gig came from the *Marlborough*." But what puzzled the investigators was how seven bodies could decompose to bones in six months. The area's perpetually cold weather should have kept the bodies in a much better state of preservation. Could it be that the skeletons had been there much longer than six months and were survivors of another wreck? Was the *Marlborough*'s gig empty when it was cast upon the shore?

Unbeknown to all involved with the loss of the *Marlborough*, the ship's name would crop up again years later. The British ship *Johnson* was steaming near Punta Arenas en route to Cape Horn late one afternoon in 1913 when her lookout sighted what appeared to be an abandoned sailing ship in the haze ahead. Her sails had long since been blown away, and the entire vessel was coated with a greenish mold or mildew. A boarding party departed from the *Johnson* for the strange ship. Closer examination revealed the vessel as the *Marlborough*. The boarding party found the deck planking sagging under their feet, doors rotting off their hinges, and skeletons scattered about the vessel. The first pile of human remains was found next to the ship's wheel. Ten others were found in the forecastle and nine more at various places aboard the *Marlborough*.

The *Johnson* discovered the derelict *Marlborough* in 1913, twenty-three years after she disappeared. The article in the *Wellington Post* offered no clue as to the mysterious reappearance of the ship. Could the *Marlborough* have been frozen in Antarctic ice during those years? Or is it possible that for twenty-three years she was drifting aimlessly about in the more remote areas of the southern oceans?

THIRTY-TWO

A Typhoon That Almost Changed the History of the United States

Much of the Devil's Sea and the far western Pacific is so empty that in the face of an approaching typhoon, there are few places where a vessel can seek shelter. Unlike the Atlantic, the Pacific Ocean allows a storm more area for expansion with fewer land masses to decelerate the winds.

A hurricane with winds reaching 150 miles an hour in the Atlantic is considered the most dangerous. Fortunately, such Atlantic storms are rare. However, typhoons in the western Pacific with winds in excess of 200 miles per hour are not rare. In fact, the greatest storm ever encountered by a fleet of warships occurred in those waters. In over five hundred years of naval history, no fleet has ever encountered winds like those that roared down on the United States Navy's Third Fleet under the command of Admiral William F. "Bull" Halsey on December 17 and 18, 1944. It inflicted more damage on ships of the United States Navy than any enemy action since the sneak attack on Pearl Harbor. It was as though Japan's legendary "divine winds" were on a rampage. It was a storm that very few of those caught in it ever expected to survive. As long as there is a United States Navy, that storm will be remembered.

It was the greatest war fleet ever assembled, fresh from its monumental victory in the Philippine Sea. But the victory had been over other human beings and their war machines.

Sunday, December 17, 1944, dawned gray and foreboding—choppy seas, gusty winds, rain squalls, and vessels in need of fuel. The ships of the Third Fleet pitched and rolled as they slammed through the heaving seas on their way to a rendezvous with a convoy of twenty-four big fleet oilers (tankers). The operation seemed but a respite from the battle of the Philippines.

Escorting destroyers, which toss in any but the smoothest seas, were gyrating wildly as fuel hoses from sluggish tankers, their decks completely awash, were dragged across cascading seas of white water and onto their pendulating decks. But there would not be much fueling that day. Some destroyers managed to get a few hundred gallons before the fuel lines ripped away from their bronze flanges. Other ships found it impossible to get fuel hoses aboard at all. Many couldn't get close enough to the plunging oilers to get a heaving line across. Each hour brought swelling walls of water cascading down on the destroyers.

Bloodied hands and eyes burning with stinging salt spray rendered the men topside nearly helpless as the decks dropped from under them. One second, the vessel would leap skyward atop an alpine heap of water. An instant later, a plunge—and those aboard would be looking up from a watery abyss. There was no end to the nautical purgatory.

The light carrier *San Jacinto* managed to get 172,000 gallons of oil (not much for a large ship of war) from the tanker *Monongahela* before the hose tore apart, covering the men of the fueling detail with oil. Even the big battleships like the *New Jersey* were being knocked about too much to transfer fuel to their escorting destroyers.

Although the winds were only twenty-six knots, the seas were tremendous, having been building up for days. Visibility was over five miles. The howling winds had no effect on the 82-degree temperature. The barometer was 29.74 and falling.

Throughout the day and into the following night, the tumultuous seas kept bearing down on the fleet. Some ships could no longer maintain their stations, for how does a helmsman steer a ship when the propellers and rudders were out of the water as often as they were in it? As dawn broke on the following day, December 18, it was evident that the great fleet lay directly in the path of a great typhoon. Existence was all but impossible for the men aboard those ships. Old sea dogs who'd been going to sea for over thirty years and had never known seasickness were too miserable to wipe the vomit from the front of their shirts. Between decks, the ship's passageways reeked with the stench of regurgitated food.

Imagine riding on the wildest of the wildest neck-snapping amusement park rides, only with the motion multiplied tenfold, and at the same time trying to carry out your shipboard duties—duties that might well save your life. Your stomach feels like it has been torn loose. Shipmates are bloodied and bruised from being slammed against bulkheads and machinery. A driving wave crushes an enclosed five-inch gun mount on a destroyer's foredeck like a crumpled beer can. A mixture of blood, vomit, and seawater slurps ankle deep in some compartments.

At 0800, the barometer read 27.30, one of the lowest readings ever recorded. Sustained winds, out of the north, were now in excess of 124 knots. Aboard some of the destroyers, it was no longer "One hand for yourself and one hand for the ship." It was "Both hands for yourself!" Not a single man in the entire fleet had ever before weathered such a storm. The ocean had gone berserk.

Then Halsey's flagship, the *New Jersey*, began receiving frantic reports. The *Dewey*: "Lost steering! Radar shorted out!" From the escort carrier *Altahama*, "Mobile crane in hanger deck broken loose! Rolling wildly, smashing everything in its path, including planes!" From the aircraft carrier *Wasp*: "Life raft off port beam, appears to have three persons aboard!" From the aircraft carrier, *Independence*: "Man overboard!" From the aircraft carrier *Monterey*, "Planes broken loose, and fire in hanger deck!" From the carrier *Kwajalein*, "Steering control lost!" From the battleship *Wisconsin*, "Kingfisher catapult plane washed overboard!" From the escort carrier *Rudyard Bay*, "Dead in the water!" From the escort carrier *Cape Esperance*, "Fire on flight deck!" From an unidentified ship, "Fuel running low!" From the carrier *San Jacinto*, "Planes on hanger deck broken loose, sliding across deck with each roll of ship. Damage severe!" Again from the carrier *Monterey*, "Fire rooms one and two abandoned due to heavy smoke from hanger deck! Ammunition being dumped overboard! Gas vapor explosion, three dead!" And from the destroyer *Dewey*, "Out of control! Losing lube oil suction! Rolling forty to fifty degrees! Radar out! Many injured! Engines stopped! Main switchboard shorted out from seawater! All electric power gone! Taking on thousands of gallons of water! Bulkheads being stove in! Bucket brigades trying to save ship!" Bucket brigades? The *Dewey*, which had valiantly fought her way out of the attack on Pearl Harbor, was now fighting for her life.

Destroyers were rolling on their beam ends, their stacks almost flat against the water. The *Dewey*'s crewmen would surely go to heaven, for they were already putting in their time in hell as she rolled 75 degrees to leeward. Breaking seas, seventy feet in height, kept rolling in on the ships.

Then came a message from the USS *Monaghan*, DD-354, a veteran of every major battle in the Pacific from Pearl Harbor to the Philippines: "Am dead in the water! Bearing 225, 1400 yards!" That was the last message ever received from the *Monaghan*. She took a roll of seventy degrees, lay over on her side, and settled beneath the frothing white water. Of her crew of 262, only 6 survived.

The USS *Spence*, DD-512, her 60,000-horsepower steam turbines dead, slid into a trough between two mountainous waves and was never seen again. Of her 317 officers and men, only 23 lived to tell of her final moments.

The typhoon had completely scattered the fleet. The *Dewey*, rolling like an inverted pendulum, lay over eighty degrees on her starboard beam—only ten degrees from being flat on her side. Tons of green and white seawater poured into her stacks and ventilation ducts.

Men prayed, some for the first time in their lives. Others cursed. Some were too busy hanging on to anything solid that they could grab to do anything else. Men aboard other ships within visibility range of the *Dewey* watched in awe as they waited for the destroyer to disappear beneath the surface. But slowly, ever so slowly, the *Dewey* began to return to upright—recovering from what was probably the greatest roll ever taken by a surviving ship.

The roar of the typhoon's winds had become silent—silent compared to the thunder of the crashing seas smashing down on the toiling ships.

Like her sister ships, the destroyer *Hull*, DD-350, which was carrying mail for the fleet, was also struggling to survive. Depth charges had torn loose from their twisted racks and were being slammed about the ship's afterdeck. Then she heaved her bow toward the crest of an oncoming wave, a behemoth of charging water as high as an eight-story building. As she settled back down, the *Hull* rolled over on her beam end. She struggled to return to a proper keel, but the wind, its velocity beyond measurement, held her down so long that water was surging in at every opening. She was past righting herself. Slowly, she settled down into the peace of the depths. For the *Hull*, the war was over. She had become a lost ship full of dead sailors and vanished hopes. Fifty-five men and seven officers out of a crew of 264 survived.

Aboard the carrier *Monterey*, smoke and fumes from her hanger deck fires were permeating the lower decks. One group of coughing and hacking sailors retreated out onto the flight deck for need of fresh air. There, in the blast of wind tearing at their bodies, five were blown overboard. Others were barely able to reach some kind of shelter.

One of the smaller ships in the storm-swept fleet was the destroyer escort USS *Tabberer*, DE-418, only six months old and with a mostly green crew. She struggled for her life, too—for she also had several seventy degree plus rolls, lost her foremast, and her crew, like those aboard the other vessels, were fighting to survive. She had lost all radio and radar contact with the fleet.

Later that afternoon, as the storm moved past the fleet and seas began to subside, the flagship *New Jersey* tallied four of her ships as lost: the destroyers *Hull*, the *Spence*, the *Monaghan*, and the destroyer escort *Tabberer*, which was missing and not answering radio calls. The surviving ships participated in what up to that time was, as Admiral Halsey described it, "the most exhaustive search in navy history." But was the *Tabberer* sunk?

Barely able to maintain steerage, her captain, Lieutenant Commander H. L. Plage, USNR, observing the situations of the *Hull* and *Spence*, somehow maneuvered his ship toward where he thought the two stricken vessels might be. During and directly after the storm, the *Tabberer* plucked survivors from those two vessels out of the frothing waters. In several instances, members of the *Tabberer*'s crew, risking their own lives, secured lines around their waists and plunged overboard to rescue struggling swimmers. In another act, riflemen aboard the destroyer escort shot a huge shark that was about to attack a swimming survivor.

As the seas began to settle, the *Tabberer*'s crew jury-rigged an antenna and was able to radio another ship, which relayed to the *New Jersey* that the *Tabberer* was about to rejoin the fleet and was carrying survivors. For its heroism, the crew of the USS *Tabberer* was later awarded a Presidential Unit Citation.

Almost 800 officers and men perished in the typhoon, including many who were washed overboard from their ships. Hundreds came near to being swept or blown into the sea. One man aboard the *Monterey* watched helplessly as five shipmates were flung over the side by the wind like pebbles from a slingshot. He recalled the scene years later: "Suddenly, I lost my footing and slid across the deck—heading straight for the ocean. There was the ocean directly beneath me and coming up fast. Instinctively, I put my heels out and luckily hit the little steel rim that surrounds the flight deck. It slowed my slide. I spun over on my stomach and luckily dropped over the edge onto the catwalk below." That sailor survived to one day become the thirty-eighth president of the United States—Gerald R. Ford.

So, the fury of the great typhoon that ripped across the western Pacific and devastated the United States Navy's Third Fleet on December 17th and 18th, 1944, came ever so close to changing the course of American history.

THIRTY-THREE

Death Under the Waves

On the afternoon of January 26, 1968, at approximately 34 degrees north latitude and 39 degrees east longitude, the newly acquired Israeli submarine *Dakar* (Hebrew for "shark") was heading east across the Mediterranean for its home port of Haifa, Israel. The 285-foot submarine was en route from Portsmouth, England, where she had just undergone complete rebuilding and modification. Commissioned into the Israeli Navy on November 10, 1967, she was a veteran of World War II service with the Royal Navy.

The *Dakar*'s 1,280 tons moved with ease at fifteen knots, forty feet beneath the storm-churned surface of the Mediterranean. For her crew of sixty-nine, there was no sense of the turbulent seas above. All was routine according to her last position report, which placed her about one hundred miles west of Cyprus. The *Dakar*'s next position report to her base at Haifa was due at 8:00 P.M.

When the base did not receive the report, there was

256

concern but not alarm. Stormy seas often interfered with submarine communications.

By dawn on January 27, however, still no word had been received from the *Dakar*. All attempts to communicate with the submarine failed. The alarm for a possibly lost submarine was given. An immediate search was initiated, in which thirty ships and dozens of aircraft from five nations participated. The water's depth at the *Dakar*'s last known position was over ten thousand feet.

While the search was getting under way, another submarine tragedy was spawning one thousand miles to the west. The French submarine *Minerva*, commanded by Lieutenant André Faure, was reported overdue. The *Minerva* had been maneuvering forty feet beneath the surface at 8:00 A.M. on January 27. She was in contact with a French air force plane directly overhead as part of a combat exercise. The aircraft radioed that she was returning to base because the surface winds were too strong to continue the exercise. The *Minerva* replied that she, too, would return to her base at Toulon, twenty-five miles to the northwest. The 190-foot submarine, carrying a crew of fifty-two, radioed an estimated arrival time of 9:00 P.M. At 9:00 P.M., however, there was no word from the sub, nor was there any response to radio messages sent to her.

At 2:00 A.M., the "overdue submarine" alarm was sounded, and a search and rescue mission commenced. Twenty surface vessels, two submarines, and a number of aircraft took part in the initial search. The boat was one of eleven submarines belonging to the 850-ton *Daphne* class. Her rated speed was eighteen knots, both surfaced and submerged. The *Minerva*'s hull was designed to withstand depths of 1,700 feet. Her last known position, however, was in water with a depth of eight thousand feet.

Fifteen hundred miles to the east, the search for the missing Israeli submarine *Dakar* was fully under way. But there was no trace of the vessel. With subsiding seas, the operation was becoming less difficult. Submarines carry emergency buoys that they can release when they are in trouble. A radio signal from such a buoy was picked up by several ships. Upon breaking the surface, these buoys automatically begin transmitting distress signals, which enable rescue vessels to home in on the transmission and find the stricken craft. From every direction, ships converged on the source of the *Dakar*'s buoy distress signals. But as they neared the area, the transmissions weakened; and when they reached the position, no submarine distress buoys could be found.

Meanwhile at Toulon, hope for the missing *Minerva* was high. The submarine had enough air supply to sustain the crew for one hundred hours. A destroyer participating in the search picked up sonar pings from what appeared to be a submarine. Before a submarine rescue vessel could reach the scene, however, the sonar pings faded away, and no trace of the *Minerva* was picked up again.

Two submarines vanishing without a trace less than 1500 miles apart in the Mediterranean within three days of each other—could this be coincidental? Or could there have been something linking the two disappearances—possibly something beyond the conception of the human mind?

Two years later, another French submarine, the *Euydice*, vanished within a few miles of the spot where the *Minerva* had disappeared.

•   •   •

Many readers will feel that the loss of the three submarines in the Mediterranean was merely part of the calculated risk that imperils all submariners. But what of a haunted submarine—a documented haunted submarine?

There have been some vessels, but not too many, that have experienced a more bizarre history than the *Scharnhorst*, *Ivan Vassili*, *Great Eastern*, and the *Ourang Medan*. One of those unlucky vessels was the World War I German submarine *U-65*. Her chronology reads like something out of *The Twilight Zone*.

The *U-65* was one of a class of twenty-four German undersea boats launched in 1916 in preparation for the kaiser's all-out campaign against Allied shipping during World War I. Like the *Scharnhorst*, the *U-65* was hexed from the day her keel was put down in the builder's yard. Within a week after her construction commenced, a steel beam slipped from a crane's sling and killed two workmen.

Some weeks later, as the U-boat was being readied for launching, three of her crew choked to death from deadly battery fumes in the engine room.

On her initial sea trial, the *U-65*'s commander made a routine checklist inspection of the boat in preparation for her first dive. A petty officer was sent to the forward part of the deck to check the movement of the bow planes. To the horror of those on the conning tower, the man walked right on past the bow planes and into the sea. His body was never recovered.

After all valves, controls, and hatches were checked and rechecked, the commander gave his first diving order on the new vessel. "Dive! Dive! Dive!" Everything functioned perfectly, and the *U-65* was taken down.

When she was resting on the bottom, routine battle station drills were carried out. Then the order to surface came. "Take her up!"

A high-pitched whirring noise from the ballast air and the sub's electric propulsion motor echoed through the hull as the crew stood by their stations, waiting for the boat to rise off the bottom. Everything seemed to be functioning as it should. But nothing happened. The main propulsion motor was revved up, put in reverse, and then forward again at full throttle. The U-65 did not move. She seemed to be stuck to the sea bottom, as though some force were holding her there. Every maneuver the commander and his crew tried failed to release the submarine from that grip.

Seawater began to seep into the hull. After twelve hours, the water in the engine room reached the level of the batteries and caused them to give off a horrible, deadly vapor. The fumes were overrunning the compartment. The engineer and his men were about to abandon and seal off that compartment. Suddenly, as though released from a giant claw, the U-65 shot up to the surface. Coughing and gagging men struggled out onto the decks, gasping for clean fresh air.

The U-65 returned to her base at Bruges for inspection and repairs. Aside from water damage to some of the batteries, the inspectors could find nothing to explain why the submarine wouldn't surface. Additional sea trials proved her to be operational. She was ordered to take on torpedoes and supplies and prepare to go out on her first patrol. As the torpedoes were being loaded, one dropped and exploded on the dock, killing the U-65's second lieutenant and five enlisted men, and bringing the number of men who died in connection with U-65 to twelve. And she had yet to meet the enemy.

One evening while the submarine was at her dock waiting for replacements for the dead crew members, an enlisted man burst into the first lieutenant's quarters screaming that he had just seen the late second lieutenant standing at the bow with his arms folded. A petty officer confirmed what the man had seen. Because of the low morale aboard the vessel, the two enlisted men were sworn to secrecy under threat of arrest. Two days later, Pederson, one of the men who had seen the apparition, deserted.

Several days later, the U-65 embarked on her first war patrol. Her area of operation was the Straits of Dover. The first day in her war zone, the U-boat sank an English freighter off the coast of Kent. It appeared that the U-65's luck might be changing.

That night, the submarine surfaced to recharge her batteries. Two lookouts, one on each side, were stationed with the first lieutenant on the conning tower. Suddenly, the starboard lookout let out a scream and pointed ahead. "Look! On the bow—it's the second lieutenant!" Both lookouts and the first lieutenant saw the apparition standing at the sub's bow.

The first lieutenant called to the figure on the bow in disbelief. "Lieutenant! What are you doing there?" The ghostlike form, standing erect with his arms folded, turned around and stared at the three men on the conning tower. The vessel's commander was summoned, and he, too, saw the spectral second lieutenant. There was no doubt among the four men that they had seen the ghost of the late second lieutenant. Then, as suddenly as he had appeared, the phantom on the bow vanished.

Even though the U-65's first patrol was militarily successful, the crew felt that they were surrounded by an aura of dread. The captain wrote in his log that the ship was haunted. The submarine returned to its base at the Bruges Navy Yard.

The boat had just docked and the lines been secured when the area fell under a barrage of Allied long-range artillery fire. The crew fled the vessel and ran to the nearest shelter at the head of the dock. The commanding officer quickly shepherded his men into the shelter and was about to step inside himself when he was struck and killed by a piece of flying shrapnel. At that instant, several of the submarine's enlisted men, who were standing just inside of the shelter's entrance, saw the phantom figure of the late second lieutenant standing at the *U-65*'s bow.

Admiral Shroeder, who was in command of the kaiser's U-boat fleet, made a personal inspection of the *U-65*. He interrogated each member of the crew. He could discover nothing. However, his questioning of the crew must have convinced him that there was something supernatural happening aboard the submarine, for before the *U-65* left for its second patrol, the admiral had a Lutheran chaplain conduct a service aboard the boat to exorcise any ghosts.

Under her next two commanders, the *U-65* ran up an impressive war record against Allied shipping. Yet the crew still felt that their ship was haunted. Several men even reported seeing the ghost of the late commander who had died in the artillery barrage.

In May of 1918, the *U-65* was patrolling the waters off the Bay of Biscay to intercept Allied ships trying to reach the west coast of France. While off Finisterre, the leading gunner, Eberhardt, went berserk, screaming that he had just brushed shoulders with the late second lieutenant. The gunner was subdued by his shipmates and placed under guard, but he managed to escape and committed suicide. That same night, the second engineer developed a high fever after breaking a leg. The next morning, shortly after dawn, a petty officer, Richard Meyer, jumped overboard and swam out of sight.

Later that same day, the *U-65* was sighted by two British destroyers and was forced to crash dive. The submarine went under an extensive barrage of depth charges. During the bombardment, an eerie greenish glow permeated the entire interior of the sub. A number of men reported having felt the presence of the late second lieutenant among them. One man said he felt a hand on his back, and when he turned around, no one was there. The *U-65* survived the attack and returned to her base.

This time Admiral Shroeder replaced the entire crew, both officers and enlisted men. After servicing, the vessel was sent back out on patrol.

On the morning of July 10, 1918, an American submarine on patrol at periscope depth in the eastern Atlantic sighted a surfaced U-boat. It was the *U-65*. As the American L-class submarine maneuvered into position, her commander noticed that the German submarine was not moving. It was wallowing out of control and drifting aimlessly. The torpedo men were standing by, waiting for the order to fire. The commander was considering surfacing and attempting to capture the enemy boat. After weighing the possibility that it might be a trap, however, he decided to torpedo the *U-65*. Raising his arm, he was about to give the order to fire when, awestruck, he watched a blast of flame gushing from the conning tower hatch. Then the entire boat erupted in flames and began to go down by the stern. As she was sliding beneath the water, the American commander, to his disbelief, saw a German officer standing at the U-boat's bow with his arms folded. As the waves were lapping at his feet, the ghostly figure turned and stared directly at the American submarine's periscope.

On July 31, 1918, the German Naval High Command issued a communique that simply stated: "One of our submarines, the *U-65*, is overdue and must be presumed lost with thirty-four officers and men."

BIBLIOGRAPHY

Almanac of Naval Facts. U.S. Naval Institute, 1964.

Baldwin, Hansen. *Sea Fights & Shipwrecks*. New York: Doubleday, 1938.

Beach, Edward. *The Wreck of the* Memphis. New York: Holt, Rinehart & Winston, 1966.

Beesley, L. *The Loss of the S.S.* Titanic. Riverside, Conn.: 7 C's Press, 1973.

Behrman, Daniel. *The New World of the Oceans*. Boston: Little, Brown & Co. 1969.

Blue Jackets' Manual. U.S. Navy Publication, 1914.

Bone, David. *The Lookoutman*. New York: Harcourt-Brace, 1923.

Brandt, Albert. "The Man Who Came Home," *Fate Magazine*, June, 1952.

Braynard F. O. & Wm. Miller. *Fifty Famous Liners*. New York: Norton, 1982.

Brown, Raymond. *Phantoms of the Sea*. New York: Taplinger Co., 1973.

Brown, Slater. *The World of the Wind*. New York: Bobbs-Merrill, 1961.

Chapman, Chas. *Piloting, Seamanship & Small Boat Handling*. Motor Boating, Inc. 1960.

Cooney, David A. *A Chronology of the United States Navy, 1775–1965*. New York: Franklin Watts, 1965.

Day, A. Grove. *Adventures of the Pacific*. Des Moines, Iowa: Meredith Press, 1969.

The Devil's Triangle. A documentary motion picture, narrated by Vincent Price, produced in 1972 by Richard Winer.

Divine, David. *Certain Islands*. New York: Arco Books, 1972.

Edwards, Frank. *Strangest of All*. New York: Ace Books, 1956.

Engel, Leonard. *The Sea*. New York: Time, Inc., 1961.

Ericson & Wollin. *The Everchanging Sea*. New York: A. Knopf, 1967.

Flyyn, Errol. *My Wicked Ways*. New York: Berkley Publishing Co., 1959.

Gaddis, Vincent H. *Invisible Horizons: True Mysteries of the Sea*. Penn.: Chilton Book Co., 1965.

Godwin, John. *This Baffling World*. New York: Hart Publishing, 1972.

Grace, Archibald. *The Truth About the* Titanic. Riverside, Conn.: 7 C's Press, 1972.

Hennessy, Tom. *Miami Herald*, April 10, 1983.

Hoehling, A. A. *A Dictionary of Disasters at Sea During the Age of Steam, 1824–1962*. London: Lloyds of London, 1962.

———. *The Great War at Sea*. New York: Thomas Crowell Co., 1965.

———. *They Sailed into Oblivion*. Thomas Yoseloff Co., 1972.

Humble, Richard. *Hitler's High Seas Fleet*. New York: Ballantine, 1971.

Lacey, Robert. *The Queens of the North Atlantic*. New York: Stein & Day, 1973.

Lauber, P. *Famous Mysteries of the Sea*. Nashville: Thomas Nelson & Sons, 1962.

Marvin, Winthrop. *The American Merchant Marine*. New York: Scribner, 1919.

Mowat, Farlet. *Ordeal by Ice*. Toronto: McClelland & Stewart, 1960.

Munroe, Ralph. *The Commodore's Story*. New York: L. Washburn Co., 1930.

Potter, E. B. "The Prisoners of the *Cyclops*," *The Naval Academy Magazine*. U.S. Navy Publication.

————— & Admiral Chester W. Nimitz. *The Great Sea War*. Englewood Cliffs, N.J. Prentice-Hall, 1960.

Potter, John Deane. *Fiasco, The Breakout of the German Battleships*. London: Pan Books, 1970.

Principal Marine Disasters, 1831–1932. U.S. Coast Guard Publication.

Randier, Jean. *Men and Ships Around Cape Horn*. New York: D. Mckay, 1969.

Riggs, J. L., *Bahama Islands*. Van Norstrand Co., 1949.

Roscoe, Theodore. *United States Destroyer Operations in World War II*. Annapolis: Naval Institute Press, 1953.

Shuster, Fred. *Los Angeles Daily News*.

Slocum, Joshua, *Sailing Alone Around the World*. New York: Century Publications, Inc. 1901.

Slocum, Victor. *Captain Joshua Slocum*. New York: Sheridan House, 1950.

Smiley & White. *Hurricane Road*. New York: Exposition Press, 1954.

Smith, C. Fox. *There Was a Ship*. Edwin Valentine Mitchell, 1930.

Smith, S. E., ed. *The U.S. Navy in World War II*. New York: Ballantine Books.

Snow, Edward Rowe. *Incredible Legends & Mysteries of the Sea*. New York: Dodd, Meade & Co. 1967.

Spectorsky, A. C. *The Book of the Sea*. New York: Appleton, 1954.

Stefansson, Vilhjalmur. *Unsolved Mysteries of the Arctic*. New York: Macmillan, 1938.

Stories of Strange Sights as Retold from St. Nicholas. St. Nicholas Magazine. Century Co., 1922.

Sweet, Nat. "The Great Eastern." *Sea Classics Magazine* Volume 3 Number 5.

Villiers, Alan. *Posted Missing*. New York: Scribner & Sons, 1956.

Wadsworth, Frank. *Nuestra Isla del Tesaro*. San Juan: Dept. de Instruccion, 1954.

Wagner, George. "THE SHIP of MISFORTUNE," *Beyond Reality Magazine*.

Westwood, J. N. *Fighting Ships of World War II*. Chicago, Follett, 1975.

Winer, Richard A. *The Devil's Triangle*. New York: Bantam Books, 1974.

———. *The Devil's Triangle*. Vol. 2. New York: Bantam Books, 1975.

———. *From the Devil's Triangle to the Devil's Jaw*. New York: Bantam Books, 1977.

——— & Osborn, Nancy. *More Haunted Houses*. New York: Bantam Books, 1981.

Numerous personal interviews with subjects and eyewitnesses.

Richard Winer writes mostly about the sea. His passion for the sea, however, sometimes succumbs to his love affair with fine vintage automobiles. His car collection includes three senior Packards from the 1930s. He is a charter member of the Classic Car Club of America. Classic cars are the subject of many of his magazine articles.

He is presently leading a drive to save the USS *Hoga*, the only surviving ship that was at Pearl Harbor on December 7, 1941, from being scrapped. If he succeeds, the *Hoga* will be permanently moored in downtown Fort Lauderdale.

Although most of his books have been on the subject of the sea, he has written three on ghosts, hauntings, and the sounds of chains dragging through the darkness. He has been working for years and years on a complete book about the mysterious U.S. Navy ship USS *Cyclops*. He has high hopes of finishing that one in this lifetime.

His home in Fort Lauderdale, where he lives with his

three dogs, is the only one in south Florida with a real railroad caboose in the backyard. He likes trains, too. He is currently researching his next book on great air mysteries.